# dBASE III Plus

## A Quick Program Reference Guide

For IBM® PC/XT/AT and compatibles

# H. J. Bomanns

An Abacus ▦ Data-Becker Book

First Printing, October 1987
Printed in U.S.A.

Copyright © 1987       DATA BECKER GmbH
Merowingerstr. 30
4000 Düsseldorf, West Germany

Copyright © 1987       Abacus Software, Inc.
5370 52nd Street SE
Grand Rapids, MI 49508

ISBN      1-55755-004-2

# Contents

- Introduction     1
- Commands     7
- Functions     82
- Network Commands     111
- Appendix A - Operators     119
- Appendix B - Fields     122
- Appendix C - Data file formats     124
- Appendix D - Config. file     127
- Appendix E - Error codes     130
- Quick Index     134
- Subject Index     141
- Index     150

# Introduction

If there is a database standard for the PC market, it's a dBase standard. More than one million copies of dBase have been sold, and it remains the best selling data management software.

Many commercial applications are based on dBase III Plus. The reasons are that dBase contains a straight forward structure and above all a sophisticated yet easy to use programming language.

Of course, there's a price to pay for this power and complexity: dBase III Plus has more than 160 commands and 70 functions. And many of the commands have multiple options. The sheer size of dBase's documentation attests to its complexity.

This Program Reference Guide presents the commands and functions very concisely. It is not an introductory manual. Instead it is a quick reference guide for the more experienced user and programmer so that he/she can find dBase information easily without having to wade through pages and pages.

# Using this guide

This guide is divided into four main parts:

> Commands
> Functions
> Network Commands
> Appendices

The entries in the first three parts are arranged alphabetically so that you can quickly locate information about a particular dBase command or function.

The Subject Index contains a list of the commands arranged by subject. This will let you identify a specific command or function that can be used for a particular database task.

Each dBase keyword can be abbreviated to the first four characters. For example: CREATE REPORT can be abbreviated to CREA REPO.

Note the following syntax conventions:

[ ]         Optional parameters are enclosed in square brackets. These parameters are not required.

<abc>       The angle brackets surround data that you must enter. Do not type the brackets.

|           A vertical bar is used to separate two alternative choices or options. You must choose one of these two parameters.

dBase keywords are printed in UPPERCASE letters.

In the following descriptions, the dBase commands and functions are presented alphabetically.

Each command or function is enclosed in a box so that it is easy to locate.

The command or function name is in the upper left corner of the box.

A brief description of the command or function is in the upper right corner of the box.

The syntax of the command or function is in the lower left corner of the box.

A more complete description of the command or function is below the box.

If a command is commonly used with another command or function  or if the explanation can be clarified by another command or function, the symbol → refers you to these entries in this guide.

# Sample Command/Function Entry

Here's a quick explanation of the format this guide uses to describe dBase's commands and functions, and their parameters:

**Command/function name**          **Brief description**

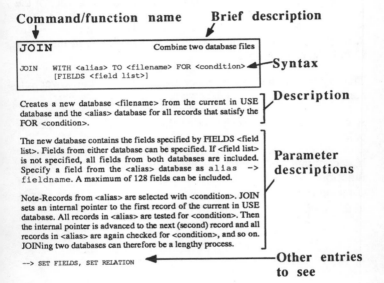

**JOIN**                         Combine two database files

```
JOIN    WITH <alias> TO <filename> FOR <condition>
        [FIELDS <field list>]
```
← **Syntax**

Creates a new database <filename> from the current in USE database and the <alias> database for all records that satisfy the FOR <condition>.  } **Description**

The new database contains the fields specified by FIELDS <field list>. Fields from either database can be specified. If <field list> is not specified, all fields from both databases are included. Specify a field from the <alias> database as `alias ->fieldname`. A maximum of 128 fields can be included.

Note-Records from <alias> are selected with <condition>. JOIN sets an internal pointer to the first record of the current in USE database. All records in <alias> are tested for <condition>. Then the internal pointer is advanced to the next (second) record and all records in <alias> are again checked for <condition>, and so on. JOINing two databases can therefore be a lengthy process.  } **Parameter descriptions**

--> SET FIELDS, SET RELATION  ← **Other entries to see**

The following conventions are used throughout the dBase III Plus Program Reference Guide.

<scope>    Unless explicitly specified, the following keywords can be used in place of <scope>:

          ALL          all records in the database

          NEXT n       the following n records in the database (including current record)

          RECORD n     only the nth record in the database

          REST         all records following the current record in the database (including current record)

<drive>    Specifies the drive identifier and optional pathname (e.g. C:\dbpath).

<condition>
          FOR <condition> refers to all records that meet the defined selection criteria.

          WHILE <condition> refers to all records from the current record pointer position forward until the selection criteria becomes false (.F.).

<field list>
          A list of desired fieldnames separated by commas.

?          Can be entered instead of a filename to list the corresponding files in the open catalog.

## CREATE\MODIFY

You can use either command to create or modify a dBase file.

To create a new file specify a nonexistent filename.

To modify an existing file specify the file of the existing file.

## TO PRINT

Redirects the output to the printer instead of the screen.

# Using the Indexes

If you know the name of a keyword, but are unsure of its usage or syntax, refer to the *Quick Index* at the back of the book. Each dBase command is listed there in alphabetical order, and refers you to the page number(s) where that keyword can be found in this guide.

If you are looking for a keyword to perform a specific task, but are unsure of its name or syntax, refer to the *Subject Index*. There you'll find a list of keywords grouped according to usage, along with short descriptions of their effects, and references to relevant page numbers.

For information and references to general dBase information and specific operations, refer to the last *Index* of the quide.

# COMMANDS

The following are the standard dBase III Plus commands.

---

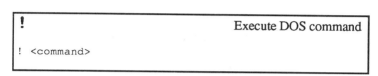

```
!                                    Execute DOS command

! <command>
```

Executes a DOS <command> COMMAND.COM must be in the current directory. The DOS SET COMSPEC command can be used to specify where COMMAND.COM is located.

--> RUN

```
*                                    Insert comment line

* <text>
```

Indicates that the program line is a comment <text>.

-->NOTE

```
?                                    Display expression

? <exp list>
```

Displays the values in <exp list> beginning on the next line.

---

**? ?**                                              Display expression

```
?? <exp list>
```

Displays the values in <exp list> beginning at the current cursor or print position.

**@...CLEAR**                                              Erase screen

```
@ <row>, <column>, CLEAR [TO] <row2>, <column2>
```

Erases the screen from screen coordinates <row>, <column> through <row2>, <column2>.

If the TO clause is omitted, the screen to the right of and below <row>, <column> is erased.

**@...SAY | GET**                              Display/input formatted data

```
@ <row>, <column> SAY <exp> PICTURE<mask>
        GET <variable> PICTURE <mask>
        RANGE <lower bound>,<upper bound>
```

Displays <exp> on the screen or printer at coordinates <row>, <column> in the format specified by PICTURE <mask>. Optionally, data can be input by the GET <variable> clause in the format specified by PICTURE <mask>.

If <variable> is a numeric or date data type, the RANGE<lower bound>, <upper bound> can specify the range of acceptable values.

<mask> in the PICTURE clause can be a function and/or a template. Functions are preceded with the character "@". Template symbols are repeated for each character to be displayed

in <mask>. If used at the same time, function and template symbols are separated by spaces.

### Functions:

| | |
|---|---|
| C | displays CR (credit) after a positive number |
| X | displays DB (debit) after a negative number |
| ( | puts negative numbers in parentheses |
| B | left-aligns numerical values |
| Z | displays 0 as a space |
| D | American date format (mm/dd/yy) |
| E | European date format (dd/mm/yy) |
| A | displays alphabetic characters only |
| ! | displays all characters, convert lower to upper case |
| R | literals are present in the mask |
| S<n> | Limit display to n characters; entries longer than <n> are scrolled within the display. |

### Template symbols:

| | |
|---|---|
| 9 | accept only digits in character expressions and digits and sign for numerical expressions. |
| # | accept only digits, spaces, and a sign |
| A | accept only alphabetic characters |
| L | accept only logical values |
| N | accept alphabetic and digits |
| X | accept any character |
| ! | convert lower to upper case |
| $ | display the dollar sign instead of leading zeros |
| * | display an asterisk instead of leading zeros |
| . | set the location of the decimal point |
| , | display only if there are digits to the left of the comma |
| Y | accept only "y", "Y", "n", and "N". Lowercase letters are converted to uppercase. |

```
--> ?, ??, CLEAR, COL(), DISPLAY, PCOL(), PROW(), ROW(),
    SET CONFIRM, SET DELIMITERS, SET DEVICE, SET FORMAT
```

---

```
@ ... TO                                    Display border

@       <row1>, <column1> TO
        <row2>, <column2> [DOUBLE]
```

Displays a border on the screen whose upper left corner is at coordinates <row1>, <column1> and lower right corner is at coordinates <row2>, <column2>.

If DOUBLE is specified, a double-line border is displayed.

--> @...SAY | GET

```
ACCEPT                              Input data from keyboard

ACCEPT [<text>] TO <variable>
```

Displays the optional <text> and accepts up to 254 characters from the keyboard and stores them in <variable>. If <text> is a literal string, it must be enclosed in quotes or brackets. <variable> must be a string data type.

--> INPUT, WAIT

```
APPEND                         Append new record to database

APPEND [BLANK]
```

Adds a new record to the end of the current in USE database.

If BLANK is not specified, then APPEND is menu assisted and you can use the full screen editor to enter the data fields.

If BLANK is specified, then an empty (blank) record is added.

--> APPEND FROM, BROWSE, INSERT, SET FORMAT TO

---

## APPEND FROM                 Copies records into database

```
APPEND FROM <filename> [FOR <condition>]
             [TYPE] <file type>]
```

Copies records from <filename> to the end of the current in USE database. The file extension of <filename> is .DBF unless the SDF or DELIMITED clause is specified in which case the file extension is .TXT. If <filename> is a dBase database, only fields with the same names and data types are copied.

<file type> can be one of the following:

> SDF      the file is an ASCII formatted file and each
>          record is terminated by a carriage return/line
>          feed sequence.
>
> DELIMITED WITH BLANK
>          the fields of <filename> are separated by a
>          blank space.
>
> DELIMITED WITH <delimiter>
>          the fields of <filename> are separated by the
>          character "<delimiter>" (enclosed in quotes).
>
> DELIMITED WITH
>          the fields of <filename> are separated by a
>          comma.
>
> DIF      <filename> is a Visicalc Data Interchange
>          Format file.
>
> SYLK     <filename> is a Multiplan formatted file.
>
> WKS      <filename> is a Lotus 1-2-3 formatted file.

--> IMPORT

11

---

## ASSIST                                    Display menu mode

```
ASSIST
```

Activates the dBASE menu system for entering commands.

The ASSIST command displays a full screen menu from which you can choose the next command to perform. ASSIST offers you a wide variety of online help.

## AVERAGE                              Calculate arithmetic mean

```
AVERAGE [<exp list>] [<scope>] [FOR | WHILE
        <condition>] [TO <variable list>]
```

Calculates and displays the arithmetic mean of the numeric fields specified by <exp list> in the current in USE database. If the <scope>, FOR or WHILE clause are omitted, all of the records in the database are used to calculate the arithmetic mean.

If the TO <variable list> clause is specified, the arithmetic means of <exp list> are saved in the corresponding variables specified by <variable list>.

--> SUM

## BROWSE                                    Edit/append records

```
BROWSE [FIELDS <field list>] [LOCK <value1>] [WIDTH
        <value2> [FREEZE <field name>] [NOFOLLOW]
        [NOAPPEND] [NOMENU]
```

Displays records of the current in USE database in row and column format (spreadsheet format) for full screen editing.

FIELDS <field list> are the name of the fields to be displayed.

LOCK < value1> specifies the leftmost number of fields that are to display as you horizontally scroll the screen.

WIDTH <value2> is the maximum length of a field to display.

FREEZE <field name> specifies the name of a field that can be edited. If omitted all fields can be edited.

NOFOLLOW applies if there is an opened INDEX file. Without NOFOLLOW, if the index field is changed, the record is reordered in the database and the current pointer is unchanged. If NOFOLLOW is specified, the record is also reordered in the database, but the current position pointer changes to the record which has replaced it.

NOAPPEND does not allow you to add new records.

NOMENU does not display the BROWSE menu

--> APPEND, INSERT, EDIT, SET, INDEX

---

## CALL                          Execute machine language program

```
CALL <module name> [WITH <character expression> |
     <variable>]
```

---

Executes the machine language program <module name> and passes <character expression> or <variable> as parameters.

<module name> must be first LOADed. The parameters are passed to <module name> in the DS and BX registers.

--> RUN

13

---

## CANCEL                                 End the application program

CANCEL

Immediately closes all open command files and returns to the dot prompt mode.

--> RETURN

## CHANGE                              Edit selected fields and records

CHANGE [<scope>] [FIELDS <field list>] [FOR | WHILE
       <condition>]

Edits records sequentially in the current in USE database. All records in the database are edited unless the <scope>, FOR or WHILE clause is used to limit the selection.

FIELDS <field list> specifies the field names to be edited. If omitted, all fields can be edited.

## CLEAR                                              Clear screen

CLEAR

Clears the screen. If any @..GET command are active, these are also deactivated.

--> @...CLEAR

---

## CLEAR FIELDS                          Delete field list

```
CLEAR FIELDS
```

Deletes the field list specified by the SET FIELDS command in all work areas.

```
--> SET FIELDS ON, SET VIEW
```

## CLEAR GETS                      Deactivate GET commands

```
CLEAR GETS
```

Deactivates all @...GET commands that were issues since the last READ, CLEAR ALL or CLEAR GETS command.

```
-->@..GET
```

## CLEAR MEMORY                   Release memory variables

```
CLEAR MEMORY
```

Releases all memory variables. Both public and private memory variables are released.

```
--> RELEASE ALL
```

## CLEAR TYPEAHEAD                      Clear input buffer

```
CLEAR TYPEAHEAD
```

Clears the contents of the keyboard buffer.

```
--> INKEY(), SET TYPEAHEAD TO
```

15

---

**CLOSE**                                    Close dBase files

`CLOSE <file type> | ALL`

---

Closes any open files of the following type:

|  |  |
|---|---|
| ALTERNATE | alternate files |
| DATABASES | databases, index files and format files |
| FORMAT | screen format files |
| INDEX | index files |
| PROCEDURE | procedure files |
| ALL | all of the above |

To close only the current in USE database, use the USE command.

`-->USE`

---

**CONTINUE**                                    Resume search

`CONTINUE`

---

Resumes searching of records that were initiated by the LOCATE command.

`--> FIND, LOCATE, SEEK, SELECT`

---

## COPY  FILE                                    Duplicate file

```
COPY FILE <source file> TO <destination file>
```

---

Makes an exact copy of the file <source file> called <destination file>.

Both <source file> and <destination file> must have the same file extension. To duplicate a database file with memo fields, you must also copy the corresponding text file (.DBT).

--> COPY

---

## COPY STRUCTURE              Duplicate database structure

```
COPY STRUCTURE TO <filename> [FIELDS <field list>]
```

---

Duplicates the structure of the current in USE database to the database <filename>. If <filename> does not exist, a new database is created. The file extension of<filename> is .DBF.

The FIELDS <field list> clause creates a new database structure containing only the fields specified in <field list>. If FIELDS <field list> is omitted, the entire structure of the current is USE database is duplicated.

--> CREATE, MODIFY STRUCTURE

---

## COPY STRUCTURE EXTENDED
                              Copy .DBF structure

```
COPY TO <filename> STRUCTURE EXTENDED
```

Creates a database <filename> which is composed of exactly four fields names: FIELD_NAME, FIELD_TYPE, FIELD_LEN and FIELD_DEC.

One record for every field of the current is USE database is created in <filename>. The records and fields of <filename> can be edited if desired and a new database can later be created with the CREATE FROM command using this structure file.

--> CREATE FROM

## COPY TO                                Copy database records

```
COPY TO  <filename> [<scope>]
         [FIELDS <field list>]
         [FOR | WHILE <condition>] [SDF]
         [DELIMITED WITH BLANK <delimiter>] |
         [TYPE <file type>]
```

Copies records from the current in USE database to <filename>. The file extension of <filename> is .DBF unless the SDF or DELIMITED WITH clause are specified in which case the file extension is .TXT.

All fields in the current in USE database are copied to <filename> unless the FIELD <field list> clause is used to specify individual fields.

All records in the current database are copied unless the <scope>, FOR or WHILE clause is used to limit the selection. IF SET DELETED ON is active, then deleted records in the current database are also copied.

The DELIMITED WITH BLANK clause separates fields with a blank space. Memo fields cannot be copied with the option SDF|DELIMITED

The following file extensions are valid for the option TYPE :

| | |
|---|---|
| SDF | Standard ASCII format (.TXT). |
| DIF | VisiCalc file format (.DIF). |
| SYLK | Mulitplan spreadsheet format (.SLK). |
| WKS | Lotus 1-2-3 spreadsheet format (.WKS). |

--> APPEND FROM, COPY FILE, COPY STRUCTURE, EXPORT

---

**COUNT**                               Count number of records

```
Count    [<scope>] [FOR | WHILE <condition>] [TO
         <variable>]
```

---

Counts and displays the number of records in the current in USE database. If the <scope>, FOR or WHILE clause is not specified, all records in the database are counted.

If the TO <variable> clause is specified, the count is saved in <variable>.

---

## CREATE                                          Create database

```
CREATE <filename>
```

Defines the structure of a database <filename>. This command is menu assisted and prompts you for the field name, data type, data length and number of decimal places.

A field name must begin with an alphabetic character and can contain up to ten characters. Field names consisting of the single letters A through J and M are reserved for alias names.

Data types can be the letters C (character), D (date), L (logical), M (memo) or N (numeric).

--> CREATE FROM

## CREATE FROM          Create database from structure file

```
CREATE <filename> FROM <strucfile>
```

Creates a database <filename> whose structure is specified by the structure file <strucfile>. <strucfile> is a file defined with the COPY STRUCTURE EXTENDED command. The new database <filename> becomes the current in USE database.

--> COPY STRUCTURE EXTENDED

## CREATE LABEL                                    Define label file

```
CREATE LABEL <filename> | ?
```

Defines a label form file <filename> for the current is USE database. This command is menu assisted. The file extension of <filename> is .LBL and is used by the LABEL FORM command to print labels.

20

When defining the label specification, the following values are allowed:

| | |
|---|---|
| Label width | 1-120 characters |
| Label height | 1-16 lines |
| Left margin starting position | 0-120 |
| Num. lines between labels | 0-16 |
| Num. spaces between labels | 0-120 |
| Num. labels across | 1-5 |

The contents of a label can be any string expressions. Non-character fields can be converted to the string equivalent using string functions (STRC(), DTOC (), etc.).

? displays a list of the current label form files in the open catalog.

--> LABEL FORM

---

## CREATE QUERY                                    Create query file

```
CREATE QUERY <filename> | ?
```

---

Defines a query file <filename> for the current in USE database. This command is menu assisted. The file extension of <filename> is .QRY and is used by the SET FILTER TO FILE command to "hide" records in a database.

The SET FILTER submenu is used to specify the field selection criteria. You can use operators (.AND or .NOT) to combine fields to form an expression.

The CONNECT submenu is used to specify multiple filter conditions.

The NEST submenu is used to specify the order of evaluation of the filter conditions.

The DISPLAY submenu applies the field selection criteria to individual records in the USE database as a way to check the validity of the SET FILTER operations.

? displays a list of the current query files in the open catalog.

```
--> SET FILTER TO
```

---

## CREATE REPORT                            Create report file

```
CREATE REPORT <filename> | ?
```

---

Defines a report form <filename> for the current is USE database. This command is menu assisted. The file extension of <filename> is .FRM and is used by the REPORT FORM command to print the report.

The OPTIONS submenu is used to specify the page heading and layout.

The GROUPS submenu is used to specify the field for which records with the same value are to be summed.

The COLUMNS submenu specifies the contents for a particular column.

The LOCATE submenu is used to find the specification of the columns based on the field contents.

? displays a list of the current form files in the open catalog.

```
---> REPORT
```

---

## CREATE SCREEN                          Create format file

```
CREATE SCREEN <filename> | ?
```

---

Defines a screen file <filename>. This command is menu
assisted. The file extension of <filename> is .SCR and is used
to create FORMAT files (extension .FMT) used by the SET
FORMAT TO commmand.

The SET UP submenu is used to specify the database and fields
for the screen file.

The MODIFY submenu is used to specify the location and size
of the screen contents.

The OPTIONS submenu is used to draw lines and boxes on the
screen and to write a .TXT file to disk.

? displays a list of the current form files in the open catalog.

```
--> SET FORMAT TO
```

---

## CREATE VIEW                            Create view file

```
CREATE VIEW <filename> | ?
```

---

Defines a VIEW file <filename>. This command is menu
assisted. The file extension of <filename> is .VUE. A view file
is used to specify a database relationship that can be recalled later
with the SET VIEW command.

The SET UP submenu is used to specify the databases, indexes
and work areas.

The RELATE submenu is used to specify the relationship
between the databases.

The SET FIELDS submenu is used to specify the fields to be displayed from a database.

The OPTIONS submenu is used to specify a filter to "hide" records in a database and a format file to be used for subsequent full screen commands.

? displays a list of the current view files in the open catalog.

```
--> CREATE VIEW FROM ENVIRONMENT, SELECT, SET FIELDS, SET
    FILTER, SET FORMAT, SET INDEX, SET RELATION, SET VIEW
```

---

## CREATE VIEW FROM ENVIROMENT
Define work environment

```
CREATE VIEW <filename> FROM ENVIRONMENT
```

---

Defines a VIEW file <filename> from the current work environment with the following contents: all open databases, index files, the numbers of the current work area, all relations, the number of the current work area, the activate filter list and any open format files.

```
--> SELECT, SET FIELDS, SET FORMAT, SET INDEX, SET
    RELATION, SET VIEW
```

---

## DELETE
Mark record for deletion

```
DELETE [<scope>] [FOR | WHILE <condition>]
```

---

Marks a record for deletion. If the <scope>, FOR or WHILE clause is not specified, only the current record is marked for deletion. A record marked for deleted can be "undeleted" with the RECALL command. A deleted record is LISTed with an *.

Records marked for deletion are removed from the database using the PACK command.

```
--> DELETED(), PACK, SET DELETED
```

24

---

## DIR                                          Display directory

```
DIR [<drive:>]  [\<path>\]  [<mask>]
```

---

Displays the directory on the specified drive. If <drive:> and \<path>\ are omitted, then the current drive and path are assumed.

<mask> can contain the wildcard characters * and ? to limit the filenames which match. If <mask> is omitted, then all filenames are displayed.

---

## DISPLAY                                       Display records

```
DISPLAY [<scope>] [<exp list>] [FOR | WHILE
        <condition>] [OFF] [TO PRINT]
```

---

Displays <exp list> for the records in the current in USE database. If <exp list> is omitted, all fields are displayed.

If the <scope>, FOR or WHILE clasues are omitted, all records in the database are displayed.

If OFF is specified, the record number is not displayed.

TO PRINT sends the display to the printer.

```
--> SET HEADING, LIST
```

---

**DISPLAY HISTORY**            Display history buffer

DISPLAY HISTORY [LAST <n>] [TO PRINT]

---

Displays the contents of the history buffer which records the commands entered at the dot prompt.

If LAST <n> is specified, the previous <n> commands are displayed.

TO PRINT sends the display to the printer.

--> LIST HISTORY, SET DOHISTORY, SET HISTORY

---

**DISPLAY MEMORY**                    Display variables

DISPLAY MEMORY [TO PRINT]

---

Displays the name, data type, value and status of all memory variables and a summary of memory statistics.

TO PRINT sends the display to the printer.

--> STORE, PRIVATE, PUBLIC

---

**DISPLAY STATUS**            Display status information

DISPLAY STATUS [TO PRINT]

---

Displays information about the current dBase working environment. The information includes:

> Database names
> Alias names
> Work area assignments
> Index filenames and key fields
> Memo filenames

Filters and formats
SET parameters
PROCEDURE file
Current DEVICE
Margin setting
Function key assignments

TO PRINT sends the display to the printer.

--> LIST STATUS

---

## DISPLAY STRUCTURE          Display database info

DISPLAY STRUCTURE [TO PRINT]

---

Displays the structure (order, name, data type and length of
fields) of the current in USE database. The number of records,
record length and date of last change are also displayed.

TO PRINT sends the display to the printer.

--> LIST STRUCTURE

---

## DO                          Execute application program

DO <filename> [WITH <parameter list>]

---

Executes the procedure or command file <filename>. If
<filename> is a procedure, it must be in the open procedure file.
The filename extension of <filename> is .PRG.

If WITH <parameter list> is specified, the <parameter list> is
passed to the procedure or command file (which must have a
PARAMETERS command).

--> CANCEL, MODIFY COMMAND, PARAMETERS, PRIVATE, PROCEDURE,
    PUBLIC

---

## DO CASE                          Execute alternative commands

```
DO CASE
```

```
DO CASE
CASE <condition 1>
        <sequence 1>
CASE <condition 2>
        <sequence 2>
CASE <condition n>
        <sequence n>
[OTHERWISE
        <sequence>]
ENDCASE
```

Selects alternative sequences of commands to be performed based on the evaluation of <condition 1> ... <condition n>.

CASE <condition 1> is evaluated and if satisfied, the <sequence 1> commands are executed. If not satisfied, the subsequent CASE <condition n> are evaluated and handled likewise. The OTHERWISE <sequence> is performed if all previous <condition>s were not satisfied.

--> DO WHILE, IF

## DO WHILE                        Execute commands repetitively

```
DO WHILE <condition>
```

```
DO WHILE <condition>
<sequence>
ENDDO
```

Performs the <sequence> of commands up to the ENDDO statement as long as <condition> is .T. When <condition> becomes .F., control passes to the statement follow ENDDO.

A LOOP command within <sequence> will immediately reevaluate <condition> to determine if the DO WHILE sequence should be executed.

An EXIT command within <sequence> will immediately pass control to the statement following the ENDDO statement.

---

## EDIT
Edit records

```
EDIT     [<scope>]
         [FIELDS <field list>] [FOR | WHILE
         <condition>]
```

---

Edits records sequentially in the current in USE database. All records in the database are edited unless the <scope>, FOR or WHILE clause is used to limit the selection.

FIELDS <field list> specifies the field names to be edited. If omitted, all fields can be edited.

--> SET FORMAT, SET FIELDS

---

## EJECT
Send printer formfeed

```
EJECT
```

---

Outputs a formfeed (Chr(12)) to the printer and sets PCOL() and PROW() to zero.

--> @...SAY, SET PRINT, SET DEVICE

29

---

**ENDDO**                                    Mark end of DO WHILE

ENDDO

This command marks the end of a DO WHILE sequence of commands.

--> DO WHILE, EXIT, LOOP

**ERASE**                                    Delete file from directory

ERASE <filename> | ?

Deletes a file <filename> from the disk directory. You must specify the file extension for <filename>. The wildcard characters ? and * are not permitted. An open file cannot be ERASEd.

? displays a list of files in the open catalog.

**EXIT**                                     End DO WHILE command

EXIT

Immediately passes control to the command following the corresponding ENDDO command.

--> LOOP

---

## EXPORT                              Copy .DBF file to PFS format

```
EXPORT TO <filename> TYPE PFS
```

Copies the current in USE database to a file <filename> in the
PFS format. The PFS format is also used by Lotus 1-2-3,
VisiCalc and Multiplan.

If a format file is open, the PFS format file contains only the
fields specified in the format file. If a format file is not open, all
fields are copied to the PFS format file.

--> COPY TO, SET FORMAT

## FIND                                    Search indexed database

```
FIND <string> | <number>
```

Searches the current in USE indexed database for the first record
with a key of <string> or <number>. A character string key
containing leading spaces must be enclosed in quotation marks.

A variable can be specified as the search key by preceding it with
the character "&".

--> FOUND() , LOCATE, SEEK, SET INDEX

## GO | GOTO                              Position record pointer

```
GO|GOTO <exp> | BOTTOM | TOP
```

Moves the current record pointer of the current in USE database.
The record pointer can be moved to record whose record number
is <exp>, to the last record (BOTTOM) or the first record (TOP)
in the database.

--> SKIP

---

**HELP**                                    Activate dBase HELP menus

```
HELP [<command> | <function> | <keyword>]
```

Displays the HELP menu for finding information about dBASE and its commands.

<command>, <function> or <keyword> can be specified to display information about a particular dBase topic.

```
--> SET HELP
```

**IF**                                    Execute conditional command

```
IF <condition>
```

IF<condition>
    <sequence 1>
[ELSE
    <sequence 2>]
ENDIF

Selects one of two alternative sequences of commands to be performed based on evaluation of <condition>. If <condition> is true, then the <sequence 1> commands are executed. If it is not true and ELSE is specified, then the <sequence 2> commands are executed. If ELSE is not specified, then control passes to the command following ENDIF.

```
--> CASE, DO WHILE,
```

---

## IMPORT                        Make .DBF file from a PFS file

IMPORT FROM <filename> TYPE PFS

---

Copies the records from the PFS format file <filename> to a
dBASE format. A format file and a view file are also created
based on the PFS file definition. After the dBASE file has been
created, it is automatically opened and becomes the current in
USE database.

--> APPEND FROM

---

## INDEX                                    Create index file

INDEX ON <exp> TO <filename> [UNIQUE]

---

Creates the index <filename> for the current in USE database.
The file extension of <filename> is .NDX.

The index is created based on <exp> (called the keyfield) which
can be a field or series of fields in the current in USE database.
The maximum length of <exp> is 100 characters. Mulitple
fields are separated by "+". Numeric and date fields must be
converted to character strings. Logical fields and memo fields
cannot be used.

Example:

>    INDEX ON zipcode + LEFT (lastname, 10) TO ziplast
>
>    The keyfield is zipcode + the first ten characters of
>    lastname.

When using the UNIQUE clause, only the first of a series of records with the same key field value is indexed. UNIQUE status remains independent of SET UNIQUE ON | OFF, even for reindexing.

```
--> DTOC(), REINDEX
```

---

**INPUT**                                              Input data from keyboard

```
INPUT [<text>] TO <variable>
```

---

Displays the optional <text> and accepts characters from the keyboard and stores them in <variable>.

If <text> is a literal string, it must be enclosed in quotes or brackets. The data type of <variable> is the same as the type of value that is entered from the keyboard.

```
--> ACCEPT, WAIT
```

---

**INSERT**                                              Insert record in database

```
INSERT [BLANK] [BEFORE]
```

---

Adds a new record into the USE database at the current record pointer.

BEFORE adds the record in front of the current record pointer.

BLANK adds a blank record into the database. If BLANK is not specified, the full-screen edit mode is used to enter the data into the new record. Data from the previous record can be copied to this record if SET CARRY ON has been specified.

```
--> APPEND, SET FORMAT
```

34

---

| **JOIN** | Combine two database files |
|---|---|

```
JOIN    WITH <alias> TO <filename> FOR <condition>
        [FIELDS <field list>]
```

Creates a new database <filename> from the current in USE database and the <alias> database for all records that satisfy the FOR <condition>.

The new database contains the fields specified by FIELDS <field list>. Fields from either database can be specified. If <field list> is not specified, all fields from both databases are included. Specify a field from the <alias> database as `alias  -> fieldname`. A maximum of 128 fields can be included.

Note-Records from <alias> are selected with <condition>. JOIN sets an internal pointer to the first record of the current in USE database. All records in <alias> are tested for <condition>. Then the internal pointer is advanced to the next (second) record and all records in <alias> are again checked for <condition>, and so on. JOINing two databases can therefore be a lengthy process.

```
--> SET FIELDS, SET RELATION
```

35

---

## LABEL FORM                     Creates labels from label file

```
LABEL FORM
        <filename> [<scope>] [SAMPLE]
        [FOR | WHILE <condition>] [TO PRINT]
        [TO FILE <filename>] | ?
```

Creates labels according to the specifications contained in
FORM <filename> from the contents of the current in USE
database. If the <scope>, FOR or WHILE clause is omitted,
labels for all records in the database are created.

If SAMPLE is specified, a printer alignment test is printed.

TO PRINT sends the labels to the printer.

TO FILE <filename> sends the labels to a disk file whose
default file extension is .TXT.

--> CREATE | MODIFY LABEL

## LIST                               List records in database

```
LIST    [<scope>] [<exp list>]
        [FOR | WHILE <condition>] [OFF] [TO PRINT]
```

Lists <exp list> for the records in the current in USE database.
If <exp list> is omitted, all fields are listed.

If the <scope>, FOR or WHILE clauses are omitted, all records
in the database are listed.

If OFF is specified, the record number is not displayed.

TO PRINT sends the display to the printer.

The LIST command is identical to the DISPLAY command
except that the output is not paused when the screen is full.

---

**LIST HISTORY**                          List history buffer

```
LIST HISTORY [LAST <n>] [TO PRINT]
```

Lists the contents of the history buffer which records the commands entered at the dot prompt. Does not pause when the screen is full. LAST displays the previous <n> commands.

TO PRINT sends the output to the printer.

The LIST HISTORY command is identical to the DISPLAY HISTORY command except that the output is not paused when the screen is full.

```
--> SET DOHISTORY, SET HISTORY
```

**LIST MEMORY**                                List variables

```
LIST MEMORY [TO PRINT]
```

Lists the name, data type, value and status of all memory variables and a summary of memory statistics.

TO PRINT sends the output to the printer.

The LIST MEMORY command is identical to the DISPLAY MEMORY command except that the output is not paused when the screen is full.

---

## LIST STATUS                    List status information

```
LIST STATUS [TO PRINT]
```

Lists information about the current dBase working environment.
The information includes:

> Database names
> Alias names
> Work area assignments
> Index filenames and key fields
> Memo filenames
> Filters and formats
> SET parameters
> PROCEDURE file
> Current DEVICE
> Margin setting
> Function key assignments

The LIST STATUS command is identical to the DISPLAY
STATUS command except that the output is not paused when
the screen is full.

---

## LIST STRUCTURE                 List database structure

```
LIST STRUCTURE [TO PRINT]
```

Lists the structure (order, name, data type and length of fields) of
the current in USE database. The number of records, record
length and data of last change are also listed.

TO PRINT sends the display to the printer.

The LIST STRUCTURE command is identical to the DISPLAY
STRUCTURE command except that the output is not paused
when the screen is full.

## LOAD                          Load machine language program

```
LOAD <module name>
```

Loads <module name> from disk. A file extension of .BIN is
assumed. The maximum size of file is 32,000 bytes.

--> CALL, RUN

## LOCATE                               Search current database

```
LOCATE [<scope>] [FOR | WHILE <condition>]
```

Searches the current in USE database for records that meet the
specified <condition>. If the <scope> FOR or WHILE are
omitted, all of the records in the database are searched.

After a matching record is found, the search can be resumed with
the CONTINUE command.

--> CONTINUE, FIND, FOUND(), SEEK

## LOOP                                  Continue DO...ENDDO

```
LOOP
```

Immediately skips to the next ENDDO command and continues
execution.

-->DO

---

## MODIFY COMMAND                    Modify command file

```
MODIFY COMMAND <filename>
```

Creates or changes the program file <filename> using the text editor. The file extension of <filename> is .PRG.

If the <filename> already exists a backup file with the file extension .BAK is also created. The maximum length of <filename> is 5000 bytes if using the built in dBase text editor. An alternate text editor is automatically used by the MODIFY COMMAND if previously specified by the TEDIT parameter of the CONFIG.DB file.

## MODIFY LABEL                              Define label file

```
MODIFY LABEL <filename> | ?
```

Defines a label form file <filename> for the current in USE database. This command is menu assisted. The file extension of <filename> is .LBL and is used by the LABEL FORM command to print labels.

When defining the label specifications, the following values are allowed:

| | |
|---|---|
| Label width | 1-120 characters |
| Label height | 1-16 lines |
| Left margin starting position | 0-120 |
| # of lines between labels | 0-16 |
| # of spaces between labels | 0-120 |
| # of labels across | 1-5 |

The contents of a label can be any string expressions. Non-character fields can be converted to the string equivalent using string functions (STRC(), DTOC(), etc.).

? displays a list of the current label form files in the open catalog.

--> LABEL FORM

| MODIFY QUERY | Create query file |
|---|---|
| MODIFY QUERY <filename> \| ? | |

Defines a query file <filename> for the current in USE database. This command is menu assisted. The file extension of <filename> is .QRY and is used by the SET FILTER TO FILE command to "hide" records in a database.

The SET FILTER menu is used to specify the field selection criteria. You can use operators (.AND or .NOT) to combine the fields with an expression.

The CONNECT menu is used to specify multiple filter condition.

The NEST menu is used to specify the order of evaluation of the filter condition.

The DISPLAY submenu applies the field selection criteria to individual records in the USE database to check the validity of SET FILTER operations.

? displays a list of the current query files in the open catalog.

--> SET FILTER TO

---

## MODIFY REPORT                              Create report file

```
MODIFY REPORT <filename>
```

Defines a report form <filename> for the current in USE database. This command is menu assisted. The file extension of <filename> is .FRM and is used by the REPORT FORM command to print the report.

The OPTIONS submenu is used to specify the page heading and layout.

The GROUPS submenu is used to specify the field for which records with the same value are to be summed.

The COLUMNS submenu specifies the contents for a particular column.

The LOCATE submenu is used to find the specifications of the columns based on the field contents.

? displays a list of the current form files in the open catalog.

--> REPORT

## MODIFY SCREEN                              Create mask file

```
MODIFY SCREEN <filename>
```

Defines a screen file <filename>. This command is menu assisted. The file extension of <filename> is .SCR and is used to create FORMAT files (extension .FMT) used by the SET FORMAT TO command.

The SET UP submenu is used to specify the database and fields for the screen file.

The MODIFY submenu is used to specify the location and size of the screen contents.

The OPTIONS submenu is used to draw lines and boxes on the screen and to write a .TXT file to disk.

? displays a list of the current screen files in the open catalog.

--> SET FORMAT TO

| **MODIFY STRUCTURE** | Change database structure |
| --- | --- |

MODIFY STRUCTURE <filename>

Changes or deletes fields comprising the structure of the current in USE database. This command is menu assisted. The structure in USE database is first copied to a backup with the file extension of .BAK. After the structure has been modified, the contents of the current in USE database is copied to the .BAK file.

If the number of MEMO fields is changed, a backup copy of the text file (file extension.$$$) is also created. If the name of a field is changed or the length of a field is aranged, the contents of that field is discarded and not copied to the modified database.

--> CREATE

| **MODIFY VIEW** | Create view file |
| --- | --- |

MODIFY VIEW <filename>

Defines a VIEW file <filename>. This command is menu assisted. The file extension of <filename> is .VUE. A view file is used to specify a database relationship that can be recalled with the SET VIEW command.

The SET UP submenu is used to specify the databases, indexes and work areas.

The RELATE submenu is used to specify the relationship between the databases.

The SET FIELDS submenu is used to specify the fields to be displayed from a database.

The OPTIONS submenu is used to specify a filter to "hide" records in a database and a format file to be used for subsequent full screen commands.

? displays a list of the current view files in the open catalog.

---

**NOTE**                                          Insert comment line

```
NOTE <text>
```

---

Indicates that the program line is a comment <text>.

```
--> *
```

---

**ON ERROR**                                      Set error trap

```
ON ERROR [<command>]
```

---

Performs <command> if a dBase error is detected. Operating system errors are not trapped.

ON ERROR without <command> disables the trap.

```
--> ERROR()
```

---

## ON ESCAPE                                    Set ESC key trap

```
ON ESCAPE [<command>]
```

---

Performs <command> if the ESC key is pressed.

ON ESCAPE without <command> disables the trap.

---

## ON KEY                                        Set keypress trap

```
ON KEY [<command>]
```

---

Performs <command> if any key is pressed. The code for key
that was pressed can be determined with the INKEY () function.
If both ON ESCAPE and ON KEY are active, ON ESCAPE has
precedence.

ON KEY without <command> disables the trap.

```
--> WAIT
```

---

## PACK                          Remove records marked for deletion

```
PACK
```

---

All records that are marked for deletion are physically removed
from the database. If any INDEX databases are opened, they are
reindexed.

```
--> DELETE, RECALL, ZAP
```

---

**PARAMETERS**                                    Accept parameters

```
PARAMETERS <parameter list>
```

Declares the variables passed to this program or from a calling program (DO...WITH).

This must be the first command in the program. The number of parameters in the DO...WITH and PARAMETERS commands must be the same. All variables are considered PRIVATE.

--> PRIVATE, PROCEDURE, PUBLIC, SET PROCEDURE

---

**PRIVATE**                                    Declare local variables

```
PRIVATE <variable list> | [ALL [LIKE | EXCEPT
        <mask>]]
```

Declares the <variable list> in this program as local. Private variables are not accessible by higher level program.

ALL LIKE <mask> declares the variables whose name match <mask> as local. The wildcard characters * and ? can be used on <mask>.

ALL EXCEPT <mask> declares all variables as local except those whose name match <mask>. The wildcard characters * and ? can be used in <mask>.

--> DO, PARAMETERS, PROCEDURE, SET PROCEDURE

## PROCEDURE                          Define routine in procedure

```
PROCEDURE <procedure name>
```

Defines the start of a routine <procedure name> in a procedure file.

<procedure name> can contain up to eight characters and must begin with a alphabetic character.

## PUBLIC                                    Define global variables

```
PUBLIC <variable list>
```

Declares <variable list> as global. Public variables are accessible by programs at any level. When a program has ended, global variables are not automatically released.

--> DO, PARAMETERS, PRIVATE

## QUIT                                              Leave dBase

```
QUIT
```

Closes all databases and returns control to DOS.

## READ                                    Activates @..GET commands

```
READ [SAVE]
```

Accepts the values and assigns them to the values variables for all @..GET commands that are outstanding since the most recent READ,CLEAR,CLEAR ALL or CLEAR GETS.

If SAVE is specified, the GETs are not cleared. If omitted, the GETs are cleared.

--> INPUT

## RECALL                                    Remove deletion mark

```
RECALL [<scope>] [FOR | WHILE <condition>]
```

Removes the deletion mark from a record. If the <scope>, FOR or WHILE clause is omitted, only the current record is unmarked.

If SET DELETED ON is specified, then RECALL ALL will have no effect.

--> DELETE, PACK

## REINDEX                                    Rebuild index file

```
REINDEX
```

Rebuilds the open index file for the current in USE database.

--> SET INDEX TO

## RELEASE                                          Delete variables

```
RELEASE <variable list> [ALL] [LIKE | EXCEPT
        <mask>] [MODULE <module name>]
```

Deletes memory variables in <variable list>.

ALL deletes all memory variables.

LIKE <mask> deletes all memory variables whose names match
<mask>. The wildcard characters * and ? can be used in <mask>.

EXCEPT <mask> deletes all memory variables except those
whose names match <mask>. The wildcard character * and ? can
be used in <mask>.

MODULE <module name> deletes a program from memory that
was previously LOADed.

--> CLEAR ALL, CLEAR MEMORY

## RENAME                                          Change filename

```
RENAME <old filename> TO <new filename>
```

Changes the name of <old filename> to <new filename>. The
name <new filename> must not already exist. An open file
cannot be renamed.

--> CLOSE, DIR, USE

---

```
REPLACE                    Change contents of selected fields

REPLACE [<scope>] <field1> WITH <exp1> [,<field2>
WITH      <exp2>...] [FOR | WHILE <condition>]
```

Replaces the contents of <field1> with the result of <exp1>,
<field2> with the result of <exp2>, etc. If the <scope>, FOR or
WHILE clause is omitted, then only the contents of the current
record is changed.

The data type of <exp1> must be the same as that of <field1>,
etc. If a numeric expression is too large for the field that it is to
replace, * are placed in the field.

--> UPDATE

```
REPORT                     Create report from REPORT file

REPORT FORM <filename> [<scope>]
       [FOR | WHILE <condition>] [PLAIN]
       [HEADING <expression>] [NOEJECT] [TO PRINT]
       [TO FILE <filename>] | ? [SUMMARY]
```

Creates a report according to the specification contained in
FORM <filename> from the contents of the current in USE
database. If the <scope>, FOR or WHILE clause is omitted, the
report is created based on all records in the database.

PLAIN suppresses the report page number and date.

HEADING <expression> specifies an additional heading.

NOEJECT suppresses an initial form feed.

TO PRINT sends the report to the printer.

TO FILE <filename> sends the report to a desk file whose
default file extension is .TXT.

SUMMARY produces a report without any detail, only summary information.

--> CREATE | REPORT, MODIFY REPORT, SET INDEX, SORT

| **RESTORE** | Read variable file |
|---|---|
| RESTORE FROM <filename> [ADDITIVE] | |

Rereads the memory variables from <filename>. The default file extension of <filename> is .MEM. This file was previously written using this SAVE command.

If ADDITIVEis not specified, the current memory variables are first CLEARed. If ADDITIVE is specified, the current memory variables are not CLEARed. Duplicate variable names are overwritten.

--> PRIVATE, PUBLIC, SAVE, STORE

| **RESUME** | Continue program execution |
|---|---|
| RESUME | |

Continues the execution of a program that was halted with SUSPEND.

| **RETRY** | Return control to calling program |
|---|---|
| RETRY | |

Returns control to the command line of the calling program. The command line is re-executed. This differs from the RETURN command which gives control to the next command line in the calling program.

51

---

**RETURN**                          Return control to calling program

RETURN [TO MASTER]

---

Returns control to the next command line of the calling program.

To MASTER returns control to the highest level calling program.

--> DO, PROCEDURE, RETRY, SET PROCEDURE

---

**RUN**                                      Execute DOS command

RUN <command>

---

Executes a DOS <command>. COMMAND.COM must be in the current directory. The DOS SET COMSPEC command can be used to specify where COMMAND.COM is located.

--> ! CALL, LOAD

---

**SAVE**                          Save current memory variables

SAVE    <filename> [ALL LIKE | ALL EXCEPT <mask>]

---

Saves memory variables to <filename>. The file extension of <filename> is .MEM and is used by the RESTORE command to retrieve the saved memory variables from the disk file.

Use ALL LIKE or ALL EXCEPT to include or exclude variables whose name is specified by <mask>. The characters ? and * can be used within <mask> as wildcard characters.

--> STORE, RESTORE

---

| **SEEK** | Search indexed database |
|---|---|

```
SEEK <exp>
```

Searches the current in USE indexed database for the first record with a key of <exp>.

Only the left most characters of the string need match if SET EXACT OFF was previously set. If a match is not found, the record pointer is set to the end of the database.

--> FIND, FOUND() , LOCATE, SET INDEX

| **SELECT** | Select work area |
|---|---|

```
SELECT <work area> | <alias>
```

Chooses one of the ten work areas in which to access a database. <work area> is identified by a number from 1 to 10, a letter from A thru J or an <alias>.

A database can be opened only in a single work area. Once opened, that work area has a current record pointer that is independent of any other work area.

--> USE

| **SET** | Display SET parameter menu |
|---|---|

```
SET
```

Displays the SET parameter menu allowing you to change any of the values. The default settings can also be SET in the file CONFIG.DB.

## SET ALTERNATE ON | OFF
Redirect screen output

```
SET ALTERNATE ON | OFF
```

ON sends screen output to the file specified by the SET ALTERNATE TO <filename> command.

@..SAY and @..GET command are not redirected.

OFF sends the redirected output to the screen.

## SET ALTERNATE TO
Open redirection file

```
SET ALTERNATE TO <filename>
```

Prepares <filename> to receive the redirected screen output when activated by SET ALTERNATE ON.

SET ALTERNATE TO without <filename> closes the file.

## SET BELL ON | OFF
Turn bell on or off

```
SET BELL ON | OFF
```

ON allows the bell to sound to indicate end of a field or error during entry.

OFF disables the bell.

Default is ON.

54

---

## SET CARRY ON | OFF
### Copy data from previous record

```
SET CARRY ON | OFF
```

ON copies the data form a previous record when using the APPEND or INSERT commands.

OFF displays a blank record during APPEND or INSERT.

Default is OFF.

---

## SET CATALOG ON | OFF                    Activate catalog

```
SET CATALOG ON | OFF
```

ON activates the catalog file that is opened by the SET CATALOG TO command.

OFF deactivates the catalog file.

Default is OFF.

---

## SET CATALOG TO                    Opens a CATALOG file

```
SET CATALOG TO [<filename>] | ?
```

Opens the catalog file <filename> and performs the SET CATALOG ON command. If <filename> does not exist, a new catalog file is created. The file extension of <filename> is .CAT.

? displays a list of the current catalog files.

SET CATALOG TO without <filename> closes the catalog file.

---

**SET CENTURY ON | OFF**          Display century

SET CENTURY ON | OFF

---

ON displays the year as a four digit number (e.g. 1987).

OFF suppresses the first two digits of the year (e.g. 87).

Default if OFF.

--> CTOD(), DATE(), DTOC()

---

**SET COLOR ON | OFF**          Enable color monitor

SET COLOR ON | OFF

---

ON switches to a color monitor.

OFF switches to a monochrome monitor.

Default is OFF.

--> SET COLOR TO

---

**SET COLOR TO**          Select color and screen attributes

SET COLOR TO [<standard>] [,<enhanced>] [,<border>
              [,<background>]

---

Selects the color and screen attributes for display.

<standard> is a pair of codes separated by / which represent the colors for normal display.

<enhanced> is a pair of codes separated by / which represent the colors for enhanced or reverse display.

<border> is a code which represent the color of the secreen
border.

<background> is a code which represents the color of the screen
background.

The codes are listed below:

| Color | Code |
|-------|------|
| Black/Gray | space\| + |
| Blue | B |
| Green | G |
| Cyan | BG |
| Blank | X |
| Red | R |
| Magenta | RB |
| Brown/yellow | GR + |
| White | W |

The following characters can be used to modify the above codes:

color monitors

| + | high intensity |
| * | blinking cursor |

monochrome monitors

| U | underline |
| I | inverse |

Example:

SET COLOR TO B/W, R+/G

Normal text is blue on white. Reverse test is bright red on
green.

--> SET COLOR ON | OFF

---

## SET CONFIRM ON | OFF    Confirm end of field

```
SET CONFIRM ON | OFF
```

ON requires you to press the ENTER key at the end of a field during full screen edit.

OFF does not require you to press the ENTER key.

Default is OFF.

---

## SET CONSOLE ON | OFF    Screen display on/off

```
SET CONSOLE ON | OFF
```

ON enables output to the screen.

OFF disables output to the screen @...SAY and @..GET commands are not affected by SET console.

Default is ON.

---

## SET DATE                                    Set date format

```
SET DATE AMERICAN | ANSI | BRITISH | ITALIAN |
         FRENCH | GERMAN
```

Set the system date to one of the following formats:

| AMERICAN | mm/dd/yy |
|----------|----------|
| ANSI     | yy.mm.dd |
| BRITISH  | dd/mm/yy |
| ITALIAN  | dd-mm-yy |
| FRENCH   | dd/mm/yy |
| GERMAN   | dd.mm.yy |

Default is AMERICAN.

--> DATE()

---

## SET DEBUG ON | OFF
Send ECHO output to printer

SET DEBUG ON | OFF

---

ON sends the output of SET ECHO to the printer.

OFF sends the output of SET ECHO to the screen.

Default is OFF.

---

## SET    DECIMALS    TO Set number of decimal places

SET DECIMALS TO <exp>

---

Sets the number of decimal places to be displayed to numeric <exp>.

Default is two decimal places.

--> SET FIXED

---

## SET DEFAULT TO
Set default drive

SET DEFAUT TO <drive>:

---

Sets the default drive to be used for all file operations to <drive>:.

--> SET PATH

## SET DELETED ON | OFF    Hide deleted records

SET DELETED ON | OFF

ON hides records that are marked for deletion from normal dBase operations. The INDEX and REINDEX, RECORD <n> and NEXT <n> commands ignore the SET DELETED ON command.

OFF allows marked for deletion to be processed.

Default is OFF.

--> DELETED()

## SET DELIMITERS ON | OFF
Display field delimiter

SET DELIMITERS ON | OFF

ON displays the field delimiter set by SET DELIMITERS TO during full-screen edit.

OFF displays the field in inverse.

Default is OFF.

--> @...GET, APPEND, CHANGE, EDIT, INSERT, READ, SET
    INTENSITY

---

## SET DELIMITERS TO          Change field delimiter

```
SET DELIMITERS TO <string> | DEFAULT
```

Changes the field delimiter for full-screen edit to <string> or DEFAULT.

DEFAULT sets the field delimiter to a colon (:). The delimiter is not displayed unless explicitly requested by SET DELIMITERS ON.

---

## SET DEVICE TO                              Set output device

```
SET DEVICE TO PRINT[ER] | SCREEN
```

Sets the output device for all @...SAY commands to either the PRINTER or the SCREEN.

Default is SCREEN.

---

## SET DOHISTORY ON | OFF
### Record program commands

```
SET DOHISTORY ON | OFF
```

ON records commands executed from program files in the history file.

OFF disables recording of program commands in the history file.

Default is OFF.

--> DISPLAY HISTORY, LIST HISTORY, RESUME, SET DEBUG, SET
    STEP, SET HISTORY, SUSPEND

---

**SET ECHO ON | OFF**          Display commands

SET ECHO ON | OFF

---

ON displays the commands executed from program files to the screen or printer.

OFF suppresses the display of commands executed from program files.

Default is OFF.

--> SET DEBUG, SET STEP, SET TALK

---

**SET ESCAPE ON | OFF**          Enable ESC key

SET ESCAPE ON | OFF

---

ON allows you to press ESC key to interrupt a command or program.

OFF disables the ESC key interrupt.

Default is ON.

--> ON ERROR | ESCAPE | KEY

---

## SET EXACT ON | OFF     Enable exact comparison

```
SET EXACT ON | OFF
```

ON requires that both <string1> and <string2> have the same characters and length in order to be .T (true).

OFF requires that <string2> be contained in <string1> in order to be .T (true).

Default is OFF.

---

## SET FIELDS ON | OFF     Enable field protection

```
SET FIELDS ON | OFF
```

ON enables the current field list specified by SET FIELDS TO <field list>. Only database fields specified in the <field list> are accessible.

OFF disables the current field list. All fields in the database are accessible.

Default is OFF.

```
--> SET VIEW TO
```

---

## SET FIELDS TO     Define field list

```
SET FIELDS TO [<field list>] [ALL]
```

The names of the fields in <field list> are put in the field list and made accessible and SET FIELDS ON is enabled.

Subsequent SET FIELDS TO <field list> commands add the new fields to the previous field list.

ALL adds the fields of the current in USE database to the field list.

SET FIELDS TO without a parameter removes the fields of the current in USE database from the field list.

The following commands ignore the SET FIELDS list: INDEX, LOCATE, SET FILTER, and SET RELATION.

--> CREATE | MODIFY VIEW, SET VIEW

---

## SET FILTER TO                    Specify filter condition

SET FILTER TO [<condition>] [FILE <filename> | ?]

---

Hides records in the current in USE database that do not satisfy <condition> or the specifications in the query file <filename>. The file extension for <filename> is .QRY.

Hidden records can still be accessed with the GOTO <number> and RECORD <number> commands.

SET FILTER TO without parameters disables the filter conditions.

? displays a list of the current query files in an open catalog.

--> CREATE | MODIFY QUERY

---

## SET FIXED ON | OFF
Set number of decimal places

```
SET FIXED ON | OFF
```

ON displays numeric values with the number of decimal places
specified by the SET DECIMALS TO command.

OFF displays numeric values based on the normal arithmetic
rules.

Default is OFF.

## SET FORMAT TO
Opens format file

```
SET FORMAT TO [<filename> | ?]
```

Uses the format file <filename> for custom forms. The file
extension of <filename> is .FMT.

SET FORMAT TO without parameters closes the format file.

? displays a list of form files in an open catalog.

--> CREATE | MODIFY SCREEN

## SET FUNCTION TO
Assign function keys

```
SET FUNCTION <exp> TO <string>
```

Assigns a string value of <string> that is automatically emitted
when function key <exp> is pressed.

Expression <string> can be up to 238 characters in length. A
semicolon (;) within the <string> indicates the ENTER key.

The default function key assignments are:

| | |
|-----|-------------------|
| F1  | help;             |
| F2  | assist;           |
| F3  | list;             |
| F4  | dir;              |
| F5  | display structure;|
| F6  | display status;   |
| F7  | display memory;   |
| F8  | display;          |
| F9  | append;           |
| F10 | edit;             |

## SET HEADING ON | OFF
Display column heading

```
SET HEADING ON | OFF
```

ON displays the column heading for each field when LISTed, DISPLAYed, AVERAGEd or SUMmed.

OFF does not display the column headings for each field.

Default is ON.

--> HELP

## SET HELP ON | OFF
Display help prompt

```
SET HELP ON | OFF
```

ON displays "Do you want some help (Y/N)" if an erroneous command is entered.

OFF does not display the help prompt.

Default is ON.

---

## SET HISTORY ON | OFF          Record commands

```
SET HISTORY ON | OFF
```

ON records the commands entered at the dot prompt to the
history buffer.

OFF disables the recording.

To review the history buffer use the DISPLAY HISTORY or
LIST HISTORY commands or use the ↑ or ↓ keys.

The number of commands that are recorded is specified by the
SET HISTORY TO command.

The default is ON.

```
--> DISPLAY HISTORY, LIST HISTORY, SET DOHISTORY, SET
    HISTORY TO
```

## SET HISTORY TO          Specify number of commands

```
SET HISTORY TO <exp>
```

Specifies that <exp> commands are to be recorded in the history
buffer.

The default is twenty commands.

```
--> DISPLAY HISTORY, LIST HISTORY, DOHISTORY, SET HISTORY
    ON | OFF
```

## SET INDEX TO
Open index files

```
SET INDEX TO <index file list> |?]
```

Opens the files in <index file list> as indexes to the current in USE database. Up to seven files can be specified in <index file list>. The default file extension for files in <index file list> is .NDX.

The first index file in <index file list> determines the order in which the in USE database is accessed.

? displays a list of the index files that are in the open catalog.

--> INDEX, REINDEX, SET ORDER USE

## SET INTENSITY ON | OFF
Display inverse fields

```
SET INTENSITY ON | OFF
```

ON displays in full screen edit fields on @...GET field in enhanced mode.

OFF displays all fields in normal mode.

--> SET COLORS

## SET MARGIN TO
Set left printer margin

```
SET MARGIN TO <exp>
```

Sets the left printer margin to column <exp>.

Default is 0.

---

## SET MEMO WIDTH TO
                                      Change memo width display

`SET MEMO WIDTH TO <exp>`

Sets the display width of all memo fields to <exp>.

Default is 50.

## SET MENU ON | OFF                    Display cursor menu

`SET MENU ON | OFF`

ON displays the menu explaining the use of the cursor keys.

OFF supresses the cursor menu.

Default is ON.

## SET MESSAGE TO                       Display user message

`SET MESSAGE TO [<string>]`

Displays <string> as the message on the bottom line of the
screen. <string> can contain up to 79 characters and is enclosed
in quotes or brackets. <string> is displayed only if SET
STATUS is ON.

SET MESSAGE TO without parameters displays only dBase
messages.

`--> SET STATUS`

---

## SET ODOMETER TO
Set odometer interval

SET ODOMETER TO <exp>

Sets the number of records between which the record count of commands (COPY, PACK, etc.) are displayed on the screen to numeric <exp>.

Default is one record.

## SET ORDER TO
Change index

SET ORDER TO <exp>

Changes the controlling index file for the currrent in USE database.

The new controlling index is <exp> which corresponds to the position of the index file in <index file list> from the SET INDEX TO command. If the value of <expression> is 0, then an index is not used.

--> NDX()

---

## SET PATH TO                                        Specify search path

```
SET PATH TO [<path list>]
```

---

Specifies the search paths to be used for all file operations. dBase searches the paths specified in <path list> that are not in the current directory. Multiple paths are separated by a comma.

The DOS PATH command has no effect on SET PATH TO <path list>.

SET PATH TO with parameters disables the new search paths.

```
--> SET DEFAULT
```

---

## SET PRINT ON | OFF               Send output to printer

```
SET PRINT ON | OFF
```

---

ON sends output to the printer. Output from the @...SAY command is not sent to the printer.

OFF redirects the output to the screen.

Default is OFF.

---

## SET PRINTER TO                          Specify printer port

```
SET PRINTER TO <device>
```

---

Specifies that the standard printer is <device>.

Valid <device>s are:

> COM1
> COM2
> LPT1

        LPT2
        LPT3

Default is LPT1.

--> SET DEVICE TO, SET PRINT

## SET PROCEDURE TO                    Open procedure file

SET PROCEDURE TO [<filename>]

Opens the procedure file <filename>. The file extension of
<filename> is .PRG.

SET PROCEDURE TO without parameters closes the procedure
file.

--> DO, PROCEDURE

## SET RELATION TO                     Connect databases

SET RELATION TO [<key expression> | <numeric
                expression> INTO <alias>]

Connects the current in USE database to the <alias> database
using either <key expression> or <numeric expression>. When
the current in USE database is repositioned, either <key
expression> or <numeric expression> is used to reposition the
<alias> database.

The <alias> database can be repositioned using <key
expression> if it is indexed. Both the current in USE database
and the <alias> database must contain that key.

72

Repositioning by record number <numeric expression> in the
current in USE database positions to the corresponding record
number in the <alias> database.

--> CREATE VIEW, MODIFY VIEW, SELECT, SET INDEX, SET VIEW ,
    USE

---

## SET SAFETY ON | OFF           Confirm warnings

SET SAFETY ON | OFF

---

ON requires you to confirm overwriting existing files.

OFF removes the confirmation requirement.

Default is ON.

---

## SET SCOREBOARD ON | OFF
                              Display status messages

SET SCOREBOARD ON | OFF

---

ON displays messages on the top of the screen if SET STATUS
is OFF.

OFF does not display messages.

Default is ON.

---

## SET STATUS ON | OFF      Display status line

SET STATUS ON | OFF

ON displays the status line at the bottom of the screen.

OFF does not display the status line.

Default is ON.

--> SET MESSAGE TO, SET SCOREBOARD

## SET STEP ON | OFF      Set single-step mode

SET STEP ON | OFF

ON executes a single program command line at a time and waits
for a response before proceeding.

OFF suspends single step execution.

Default is OFF.

--> SET DEBUG, SET ECHO

## SET TALK ON | OFF      Display command result

SET TALK ON | OFF

ON displays any messages that results from the execution of a
command.

OFF suspends the display.

Default is OFF.

---

## SET TITLE ON | OFF                    Prompt for title

SET TITLE ON | OFF

---

ON prompts you to enter a descriptive title into the open catalog.

OFF supresses the prompt.

Default is ON.

--> EDIT, SET CATALOG

---

## SET TYPEAHEAD TO                Set size of input buffer

SET TYPEAHEAD TO <exp>

---

Sets the length of the typeahead buffer to numeric <exp>. A value of 0 disables the typeahead buffer. The maximum length is 32000.

Default is 20.

---

## SET UNIQUE ON | OFF                    Allow unique keys

SET UNIQUE ON | OFF

---

ON prevents records having identical keys from being added to the index. This command is the same as INDEX ON.. TO.. UNIQUE.

OFF allows duplicate keys in the index.

Default is OFF.

--> REINDEX, SET INDEX

---

## SET VIEW TO                                Open view file

```
SET VIEW TO <filename> | ?
```

Opens a view file <filename> which sets up access to a previous
set of databases. The file extension of <filename> is .VUE.

The view file was saved with a CREATE|MODIFY VIEW
command and contains specifications corresponding to:

> SELECT
> USE...INDEX...
> SET RELATION TO
> SET FIELDS TO
> SET FORMAT TO

? displays a list of view files in the catalog file.

```
--> CREATE VIEW FROM ENVIRONMENT, CREATE VIEW| MODIFY VIEW,
    SET FIELDS, SET FILTER, SET FORMAT, SET RELATION
```

## SKIP                    Move record pointer forward or backward

```
SKIP <exp>
```

Moves the record pointer by numeric <exp> from the current
record pointer. If <exp> is omitted, the record pointer is moved
forward by one record.

If the current in USE database is indexed, SKIP moves the record
pointer in indexed order.

```
--> BOF(), GO | GOTO, EOF(), RECNO()
```

---

## SORT                                          Create sorted copy of database

SORT    [<scope>] ON <field name> [/A] [/C] [/D]
        [FOR | WHILE <condition>] TO <filename>

A/      sorts in ascending order
D/      sorts in descending order
C/      does not distinguish between upper and lower case and
        can be used with A/ or D/.

---

Creates a new reordered database <filename> from the current in
USE database. The new database is reordered based on the
contents of <field name> and one of the three flags (/A,/S, and
/D).

The contents of the new database can be limited by <scope> and
WHILE <condition> clauses.

Up to ten <field names> can be specified, separated by commas.
Logical and memo fields cannot be sorted. <filename> cannot
specify the current in USE or any other open database.

If a flag is omitted, the records are sorted in ascending (/A) order.

--> INDEX

---

## STORE                                            Assign value to variable

STORE <exp> TO <variable list>

---

Assigns the value of <exp> to <variable list>.

If a field has the same name as a memory variable the field has
precedence in all operation. To explicitly refer to the memory
variable, use the notation m-> <variable>. This command
is similar to <variable>=<exp> except that <exp> can be
assigned to multiple variables at one time.

---

**SUM**                              Sum the values of numeric fields

```
SUM      [<scope>] [<expression list>]
         [TO <variable list>]
         [FOR | WHILE <condition>]
```

---

Calculates and displays the sum of the numeric values in
<expression list> for the records in the current in USE database.
If <expression list> is omitted, all numeric fields in the database
are summed.

If the <scope>, FOR or WHILE clause are omitted, the numeric
values from all records of the database are summed.

If TO <variable list> is specified, the sums are stored in
<variable list>.

--> AVERAGE, TOTAL

---

**SUSPEND**                              Halt program execution

```
SUSPEND
```

---

Halts the execution of a program. The program can also be
halted by pressing the ESC key.

--> CANCEL, HISTORY, RETURN

---

| **TEXT** | Display block of text |
|---|---|

```
TEXT
```

> TEXT
> <text lines>
> ENDTEXT

Displays the <text lines> on the screen or printer. All <text lines> between TEXT and ENDTEXT are displayed.

```
--> SET DEVICE
```

---

| **TOTAL** | Create totals file |
|---|---|

```
TOTAL <scope> ON <key field> [FIELDS <field list>]
        [FOR | WHILE <condition>] TO <filename>
```

---

Creates a new database <filename> containing the subtotals of the numeric fields specified by FIELDS <field list> from the current in USE database. If the FIELDS <field list> is omitted, all numeric fields are subtotaled.

The current in USE database must either be INDEXED or sorted on <key field>. Either or both <scope> and <condition> can be used to limit the records whose fields are to be subtotaled.

```
--> INDEX, SET INDEX TO, SORT, SUM
```

---

| **TYPE** | Display ASCII files |
|---|---|

```
TYPE <filename> [TO PRINT]
```

Displays the contents of the ASCII file <filename>.

<filename> must include the filename extension and the drive and/or pathname if <filename> is not on the current drive and path.

TO PRINT sends the display to the printer.

| **UPDATE** | Update from another database |
|---|---|

```
UPDATE ON <key field> FROM <alias> REPLACE <field>
          WITH <exp1> [,<field2> WITH <exp2>…]
          [RANDOM]
```

Changes fields in the current in USE database with the contents of the database <alias>. Both databases must be either INDEXed or SORTed on <key field> unless RANDOM is specified. Then, <alias> can be in any order, but must contain <key field>. If the <key field> is non-unique, only the first occurance is updated!

The contents <field1> is replaced by <exp1>, <field2> by <exp2>, etc. To specify a field in the alias file, use the expression alias -> fieldname.

--> REPLACE, SET INDEX, SORT

---

```
USE                                                Open database

USE    [<filename>] [INDEX <index list>]
       [ALIAS <alias name>] | ?
```

Opens the database <filename> in the current work area. If the INDEX <index list> clause is included, the specified index files are also opened.

ALIAS <alias name> assigns an alias name to the current work area.

USE without parameters closes the current in USE database and any associated index files.

? display a list of the databases in the open catalog.

--> CLOSE, INDEX, SELECT, SET INDEX, SET VIEW

```
WAIT                                           Interrupt processing

WAIT [<text>] [TO <variable>]
```

Displays optional <text> and waits for a single key to be pressed which is then assigned to <variable>.

If <text> is omitted, dBase displays "Press any key to continue."

```
ZAP                                              Delete all records

ZAP
```

Deletes all records in the current in USE database. This command corresponds to DELETE ALL followed by PACK, but is faster.

# FUNCTIONS

The following are the standard dBase III Plus functions:

* indicates that no parameters are required.

---

| **&** | Substitute macro |
|---|---|

```
& <stringvar>
```

Input type: variable name
Output type: character, date, logical or numeric value

Returns the contents of <stringvar>.

Example:

>       USE db INDEX dbadx
>       STORE 'ABC' TO keyfld
>       FIND &keyfld
>
>       Searches indexed database db for a key of 'ABC'.

| **ABS** | Return absolute value |
|---|---|

```
ABS (<exp>)
```

Input type: numeric expression
Output type: numeric value

Returns the absolute value for the numeric <exp>.

---

## ASC                                    Convert character to ACSII code

ASC (<exp>)

---

Input type: character string
Output type: numeric value

Returns the ASCII code of the first character of the string
<exp>.

---

## AT                                   Find starting position of substring

AT (<expl>, <exp2>)

---

Input type: character string
Output type: numeric value

Returns the starting position of string <expl> within string
<exp2>. Returns 0 if <expl> is not contained in <exp2>.

Example:

        STORE 'ABCDEFG' to alpha
        ? AT ('D', alpha)
             4

--> SUBSTR(), LEFT(), RIGHT()

**BOF**                                        Beginning of file?

BOF ()

Input type: *
Output type: logical

Returns .T. when a command tries to position the record pointer in front of the first logical record in the current in USE database; otherwise returns .F.

--> EOF()

**CDOW**                              Convert date to day of week

CDOW (<exp>)

Input type: date expression
Output type: character string

Returns the name of the day of the week (Monday, Tuesday, etc.) corresponding to the date <exp>. <exp> must be a date data type.

--> DOW(), DAY()

**CHR**                         Convert ASCII code to character code

CHR (<exp>)

Input type: numeric expression
Output type: character

Returns the character corresponding to the numeric ASCII code <exp>.

84

---

## CMONTH
Convert date to month

CMONTH (<exp>)

---

Input type: date expression
Output type: character string

Returns the name of the month (January, February, etc.)
corresponding to the date <exp>. <exp> must be a date data
type.

--> MONTH()

---

## COL
Return column number of cursor

COL()

---

Input type: *
Output type: numeric value

Returns the column number of the current cursor position.

--> ROW()

---

## CTOD
Convert string to date variable

CTOD (<exp>)

---

Input type: character string
Output type: date variable

Returns a date variable from a string <exp> in the form
"mm/dd/yy".

--> DTOC()

---

## DATE                                              Return system date

DATE()

---

Input type: *
Output type: date variable

Returns the system date as a date data type in the format
mm/dd/yy unless changed by the SET DATE or SET
CENTURY commands.

--> SET CENTURY, SET DATE

---

## DAY                                         Return day of the month

DAY (<exp>)

---

Input type: date expression
Output type: numeric value

Returns the calender day (1,2,...31) corresponding to the date
<exp>. <exp> must be a date data type.

--> CDOW(), DOW()

---

## DBF                                      Return current database name

DBF()

---

Input type: *
Output type: character string

Returns the name of the current in USE database. Returns a null
string if no database is open in the current work area.

--> NDX()

## DELETED
Deleted record?

```
DELETED()
```

Input type: *
Output type: logical

Returns .T. if the current record is marked as deleted; otherwise returns .F.

```
--> SET DELETED ON
```

## DISKSPACE
Return amount of disk space

```
DISKSPACE()
```

Input type: *
Output type: numeric value

Returns the number of bytes of unused disk space available on the current default drive.

```
--> SET DEFAULT
```

## DOW
Return day of the week

```
DOW (<exp>)
```

Input type: date expression
Output type: numeric value

Returns a number (1=Sunday, 2=Monday,...7=Saturday, etc.) corresponding to the date <exp>. <exp> must be a date data type.

```
--> CDOW(), DAY()
```

---

## DTOC
Convert date variable to string

DTOC (<exp>)

---

Input type: date variable
Output type: character string

Returns a character string in the format "mm/dd/yy" corresponding to the date variable <exp>.

--> CTOD(), SET CENTURY, SET DATE

---

## EOF
End of file?

EOF()

---

Input type: *
Output type: logical

Returns .T. when a command tries to position the record pointer beyond the last logical record in the current in USE database; otherwise returns .F.

--> BOF()

---

## ERROR
Return error code

ERROR()

---

Input type: *
Output type: numeric value

Returns the error code for any outstanding error condition. Returns 0 if no error condition is outstanding.

See the Appendix E for a list of Error Codes.

---

## EXP                                    Return exponentiation function

EXP (<exp>)

---

Input type: numeric expression
Output type: numeric value

Returns the value of *e* raised to the <exp> power.

---

## FIELD                                             Return fieldname

FIELD(<exp>)

---

Input type: numeric expression
Output type: character

Returns the name of the field corresponding to the field's
position <exp> (from 1 to 128) in the current in USE database.
Returns a null string if a field is not in the specified position in
the database.

---

## FILE                                             Does file exists?

FILE(<filename>)

---

Input type: character string
Output type: logical

Returns .T. if <filename> already exists in the current search
path; otherwise returns .F.

<filename> must include the file extension.

--> SET PATH

89

---

## FKLABEL                          Function key assignment

FKLABEL (<exp>)

Input type: numeric expression
Output type: character string

Returns a character string (e.g. F1) corresponding to the function
key specified by numeric <exp>.

--> SET FUNCTION

## FKMAX                            Number of function keys

FKMAX ()

Input type: *
Output type: numeric value

Returns the number of available programmable function keys.

--> FKLABEL(), SET FUNCTION

## FOUND                           Result of search operation

FOUND ()

Input type: *
Output type: logical

Returns .T. if result of the last FIND, SEEK, LOCATE or
CONTINUE command was successful; otherwise returns .F.

---

## GETENV                              Environment variable from DOS

GETENV (<exp>)

---

Input type: character string
Output type: character string

Returns the value of the DOS environmental variable <exp>.

--> OS(), VERSION()

---

## IIF                                              Immediate IF

IIF (<condition>, <exp1>, <exp2>)

---

Input type: character, date or numeric expression
Output type: character, date or numeric value

Returns the result of <exp1> if <condition> is true; otherwise
returns the result of <exp2>. Both <exp1> and <exp2> must be
of the same data type.

--> IF

---

## INKEY                     Return ASCII code of the last key pressed

INKEY ()

---

Input type: *
Output type: numeric value

Returns the ASCII value of the first character in the typeahead
buffer. Returns 0 if the typeahead buffer is empty.

The follows are the codes returned by INKEY() for special keys:

| Special key | Code |
|-------------|------|
| Ctrl/cursor left | 26 |
| Ctrl/cursor right | 2 |
| Ctrl/End | 23 |
| Ctrl/Home | 29 |
| Ctrl/PgDn | 30 |
| Ctrl/PgUp | 31 |
| Cursor down | 24 |
| Cursor left | 19 |
| Cursor right | 4 |
| Cursor up | 5 |
| Del | 7 |
| End | 6 |
| Home | 1 |
| Ins | 22 |
| PgDn | 3 |
| PgUp | 18 |

--> CHR(), ON KEY, READKEY() SET TYPEAHEAD,

---

# INT                                        Return integer

INT (<exp>)

---

Input type: numeric expression
Output type: numeric value

Returns the integer portion of numeric <exp> without rounding.

## ISALPHA

Is first character alphabetic?

ISALPHA (<exp>)

Input type: character string
Output type: logical

Returns .T. if the first character of string <exp> is alphabetic;
otherwise returns .F.

--> ISLOWER(), ISUPPER(), LOWER(), UPPER()

## ISCOLOR

Is screen display color mode?

ISCOLOR()

Input type: *
Output type: logical

Returns .T. if the screen display is in color mode; otherwise
returns .F.

--> COLOR

## ISLOWER

Is first character lowercase?

ISLOWER (<exp>)

Input type: character string
Output type: logical

Returns .T. if the first character of string <exp> is a lowercase
letter; otherwise returns .F.

--> ISALPHA(), ISUPPER(), LOWER(), UPPER()

---

## ISUPPER                          Is first character uppercase?

ISUPPER(<exp>)

Input type: character
Output type: logical

Returns .T. if the first character of string <exp> is an uppercase
letter; otherwise returns .F.

--> ISALPHA(), ISLOWER(), LOWER(), UPPER()

## LEFT                             Extract leftmost characters

LEFT (<exp>,<n>)

Input type: character string
Output type: character string

Returns the leftmost <n> characters of string <exp>. Returns
null string if <n> is 0.

Example:

        STORE 'ABCDEFG' TO alpha
        ? LEFT (alpha,2)
        AB

--> AT(), RIGHT(), SUBSTR()

---

## LEN
Return length of string

`LEN (<exp>)`

Input type: character string
Output type: numeric value

Returns the number of characters in the string <exp>.

---

## LOG
Return natural logarithm

`LOG (<exp>)`

Input type: numeric expression
Output type: numeric value

Returns the natural logarithm for the numeric <exp>.

`--> EXP ()`

---

## LOWER
Convert upper to lowercase

`LOWER (<exp>)`

Input type: character string
Output type: character string

Returns a string in which all uppercase characters of string <exp> have been changed to lowercase characters.

Example:

        STORE 'abcDEF' TO alpha
        ? LOWER (alpha)
        abcdef

`--> ISALPHA(), ISLOWER(), ISUPPER(), UPPER()`

---

## LTRIM                                              Remove leading blanks

LTRIM <exp>

Input type: character string
Output type: character string

Returns a string in which all leading blank spaces in string <exp> have been removed.

--> RTRIM(), TRIM()

## LUPDATE                          Return date of the last database update

LUPDATE()

Input type: *
Output type: date

Returns a date variable whose value is the date on which the current in USE database was last changed.

## MAX                                              Return larger of two values

MAX (<exp1>, <exp2>)

Input type: numeric expression
Output type: numeric value

Returns the larger of the two numeric <exp1> and <exp2>.

--> MIN()

---

## MESSAGE
Return error message

`MESSAGE()`

---

Input type: *
Output type: character string

Returns the textual error message for the current error condition.
Returns a null string if no error condition is outstanding.

--> ERROR()

---

## MIN
Return smaller of two values

`MIN(<exp1>, <exp2>)`

---

Input type: numeric expression
Output type: numeric value

Returns the smaller of the two numeric <exp1> and <exp2>.

--> MAX()

---

## MOD
Return remainder of division

`MOD(<exp1>, <exp2>)`

---

Input type: numeric expression
Output type: numeric value

Returns the remainder of the division of numeric <exp1> by
<exp2> (modulo division). The sign of the value returned is the
same as the sign of <exp2>.

## MONTH                                    Return the month

```
MONTH (<exp>)
```

Input type: date expression
Output type: numeric value

Returns a number (1=January, 2=February,...12=December, etc.)
corresponding to the month of date <exp>. <exp> must be a
date data type.

```
--> CMONTH(), DAY(), YEAR()
```

## NDX                                       Return index name

```
NDX (<exp>)
```

Input type: numeric expression
Output type: character string

Returns the name of the open index database in the <exp>
position of the index list (as specified by the SET INDEX TO or
USE...INDEX commands).

## OS                                       Operating system name

```
OS ()
```

Input type: *
Output type: character string

Returns the name of the operating system.

---

## PCOL                                    Return printer column position

PCOL()

---

Input type: *
Output type: numeric value

Returns the column number of the current printer position.

--> PROW()

## PROW                                      Return printer line position

PROW()

---

Input type: *
Output type: numeric value

Returns the row number of the current printer position.

--> PCOL(),

## READKEY                                              Return key code

READKEY()

---

Input type: *
Output type: numeric value

Returns the code corresponding to the key that was pressed to
exit a full screen edit command (APPEND, BROWSE,
CHANGE, CREATE, EDIT, INSERT, MODIFY, and READ).

List of READKEY codes:

| Key | Code (data unchanged) | Code (data changed) | Purpose |
|---|---|---|---|
| Crtl-End | - | 270 | exit, save |
| Ctrl-W | - | 270 | exit, save |
| Backspace | 0 | 256 | move back one char. |
| Ctrl-H | 0 | 256 | move back one char. |
| Ctrl-S | 0 | 256 | move back one char. |
| Ctrl-D | 1 | 257 | move forward one char. |
| Ctrl-L | 1 | 257 | move forward one char. |
| Ctrl-A | 2 | 258 | move back one word |
| Home | 2 | 258 | move back one word |
| Ctrl-F | 3 | 259 | move forward one word |
| End | 3 | 259 | move forward one word |
| ↑ | 4 | 260 | move back one field |
| Ctrl-E | 4 | 260 | move back one field |
| Ctrl-K | 4 | 260 | move back one field |
| ↓ | 5 | 261 | move forward one field |
| Ctrl-J | 5 | 261 | move forward one field |
| Ctrl-R | 6 | 262 | move back one screen |
| PgUp | 6 | 262 | move back one screen |
| Ctrl-C | 7 | 263 | move forward one screen |
| PgDn | 7 | 263 | move forward one screen |
| Ctrl-Q | 12 | - | exit, don't save |
| Esc | 12 | - | exit, don't save |
| Ctrl-M | 15 | 271 | RETURN |
| Ctrl-Home | 33 | 289 | exit, save |
| F1 | 36 | 292 | HELP |

--> READKEY(), ON KEY

---

## RECCOUNT                    Return number of records in database

RECCOUNT ()

---

Input type: *
Output type: numeric value

Returns the number of records in the current in USE database.
Returns 0 if no file is in USE.

The SET DELETED and SET FILTER commands do not
change the count of records.

--> RECSIZE()

## RECNO                        Return current record number

RECNO ()

---

Input type: *
Output type: numeric value

Returns the record number of the current record in the USE
database.

Returns 1 if EOF() is .T. and there are no records in the
database.

Returns 0 if no database is in USE.

--> RECCOUNT(), RECSIZE()

## RECSIZE                              Return record length

RECSIZE()

Input type: *
Output type: numeric value

Returns the length of a record in the current in USE database.

Returns 0 if no database is in USE.

--> RECCOUNT()

## REPLICATE                           Copies a string n times

REPLICATE (<exp>,<n>)

Input type: character string
Output type: character string

Returns a string in which string <exp> has been repeated <n> times. The maximum length of the resulting string cannot exceed 254 characters.

Example:

        STORE 'ABC' TO alpha
        ? REPLICATE (alpha,3)
        ABCABCABC

102

# RIGHT

Extract rightmost characters

`RIGHT (<exp>,<n>)`

Input type: character string
Output type: character string

Returns the rightmost <n> characters of the string <exp>.
Returns a null string if <n> is 0. Returns <exp> if <n> is
greater than the length of string <exp>.

Example:

>        STORE 'ABCDEF' TO alpha
>        ? RIGHT (alpha,3)
>        DEF

--> AT(), LEFT(), SUBSTR()

# ROUND

Round numeric value

`ROUND (<exp>, <p>)`

Input type: numeric expression
Output type: numeric value

Returns a value corresponding to <exp> rounded to <p> decimal
places.

If <p> is positive, this is the number of places after the decimal
point. If <p> is negative, this is the number of places before the
decimal point.

---

## ROW                                    Return line number of cursor

ROW()

Input type: *
Output type: numeric value

Returns the row number of the current cursor position.

--> @...SAY | GET, COL()

## RTRIM                                       Remove trailing blanks

RTRIM <exp>

Input type: character string
Output type: character string

Returns a string in which all trailing blank spaces in string <exp> have been removed.

--> LTRIM(), TRIM()

## SPACE                                         Return string of blanks

SPACE (<n>)

Input type: numeric expression
Output type: character string

Returns a string of <n> blank spaces. The maximum value of <n> is 254.

--> REPLICATE()

---

## SQRT
Return square root

SQRT (<exp>)

Input type: numeric expression
Output type: numeric value

Returns the square root of numeric <exp>. <exp> must be a positive number.

--> SET DECIMALS, SET FIXED

---

## STR
Convert numeric variable to string

STR (<exp> [, <n> [,<d>]])

Input type: numeric expression
Output type: character string

Returns a character string corresponding to the numeric <exp>. The character string has a length of <n> characters with <d> decimal places. If <n> is omitted, length is 10. If <d> is omitted, decimal places is 0.

---

## STUFF
Replace characters in string

STUFF (<exp1>, <start>, <n>, <exp2>)

Input type: character string
Output type: character string

Returns a string <exp1> in which the characters starting at position <start> for a length of <n> have been replaced with the characters of string <exp2>. If <n> is zero, the characters are inserted without replacements.

Example:

>       STORE 'ABCDEF' TO alpha
>       ? STUFF (alpha, 2,3, 'zzz')
>       AzzzEF

--> LEFT(), RIGHT(), SUBSTR()

## SUBSTR                                          Extract substring

```
SUBSTR (exp>, <start> [,<n>]
```

Input type: character string
Output type: character string

Returns a string composed of the <n> characters starting at
position <start> of string <exp>. Returns the entire substring
beginning at position <start> of the string <exp> if <n> is
omitted.

--> LEFT(), RIGHT(), STUFF()

## TIME                                            Return system time

```
TIME ()
```

Input type: *
Output type: character string

Returns the system time in the format "hh:mm:ss".

## TRANSFORM

Convert to PICTURE format

TRANSFORM (<exp>, <mask>)

Input type: numeric or character string
Output type: character string

Returns a string from <exp> that has been formatted by
PICTURE <mask>. <exp> can be either a string expression or a
numeric expression.

<mask> can be a function and/or a template. Functions are
preceded with the character "@". Template symbols are repeated
for each character to be displayed in <mask>. If used at the same
time, function and template symbols are separated by spaces.

**Functions:**

| | |
|---|---|
| C | displays CR (credit) after a positive number |
| X | displays DB (debit) after a negative number |
| ( | puts negative numbers in parentheses |
| B | left-aligns numerical values |
| Z | displays 0 as a space |
| D | American date format (mm/dd/yy) |
| E | European date format (dd/mm/yy) |
| A | displays alphabetic characters only |
| ! | displays all characters, convert lower to upper case |
| R | literals are present in the mask |
| S<n> | Limit display to <n> characters; entries longer the <n> are scrolled within the display. |

## Template symbols:

| | |
|---|---|
| 9 | accept only digits in character expressions and digits and sign for numerical expressions. |
| # | accept only digits, spaces, and a sign |
| A | accept only alphabetic characters |
| L | accept only logical values |
| N | accept alphabetic and digits |
| X | accept any character |
| ! | convert lower to upper case |
| $ | display the dollar sign instead of leading zeros |
| * | display an asterisk instead of leading zeros |
| . | set the location of the decimal point |
| ' | display only if there are digits to the left of the comma |
| Y | accept only "y","Y", "n", and "N". Lowercase letters are converted to uppercase. |

## TRIM                                           Remove trailing blanks

TRIM (<exp>)

Input type: character string
Output type: character string

Returns a string in which all trailing blank spaces in string
<exp> have been removed.

--> LTRIM(), RTRIM()

---

## TYPE
Return data type

```
TYPE ('<variable>')
```

Input type: character, numerical, logical, memo expression
Output type: single character

Returns a code corresponding to the data type of a <variable>:

|   |           |
|---|-----------|
| C | character |
| L | logical   |
| M | memo      |
| N | numeric   |
| U | undefined |

## UPPER
Convert lower to uppercase

```
UPPER (<exp>)
```

Input type: character string
Output type: character string

Returns a string in which all lowercase characters of string <exp> have been changed to uppercase characters.

--> ISLOWER(), ISUPPER(), LOWER()

---

## VAL
Convert string to numeric variable

VAL (<exp>)

Input type: character string
Output type: numeric value

Returns a numeric variable corresponding to the character string <exp>. Returns 0 if <exp> contains non-numeric characters.

The number of decimal places in the numeric variables is determined by the SET DECIMALS command.

## VERSION
Return dBase version

VERSION ()

Input type: *
Output type: character string

Returns the version of dBase III Plus.

## YEAR
Return year

YEAR <exp>

Input type: date expression
Output type: numeric value

Returns the four digit year (e.g. 1987) corresponding to the date <exp>. A four digit year is returned regardless of the SET CENTURY command.

# Network Commands

The following commands are additions or changes to the standard dBase III Plus commands specifically for the Network version, dBase ADMINSTRATOR.

---

| CHANGE | Edit selected fields and records |
|---|---|

```
CHANGE [<scope>] [FIELDS <field list>] [FOR|WHILE
       <condition>]
```

Edits records sequentially in the current in USE database. All records in the database are edited unless the <scope>, FOR, or WHILE clause is used to limit the selection.

FIELDS <field list> specifies the field names to be edited. If omitted, all fields can be edited.

One of the following messages appears in the status bar of the CHANGE menu to indicate the disposition of the command:

```
Exclusive use
File locked
Read only
Record locked
Record unlocked
```

---

## DISPLAY STATUS          Display status information

```
DISPLAY STATUS
```

Displays information about the current dBase working environment this includes:

>    database names
>    alias names
>    work area assignments
>    index file and key fields
>    memo filenames
>    filters and formats
>    SET parameters including SET ENCRYPTION
>        and SET EXCLUSIVE
>    PROCEDURE file
>    current DEVICE
>    margin setting
>    function key assignments

## DISPLAY USERS  Display logged on work stations

```
DISPLAY USERS
```

Displays the names of all logged on work stations.

## LIST STATUS                    List status information

```
LIST STATUS
```

Lists information about the current dBase working environment. This includes:

>    database names
>    alias names
>    work area assignments

112

index filenames and key fields
memo filenames
filters and formats
SET parameters including SET ENCRYPTION
    and SET EXCLUSIVE
PROCEDURE file
current DEVICE
margin setting
function key assignments

The LIST STATUS command is identical to the DISPLAY STATUS command except that the list is not paused when the screen is full.

---

## LOGOUT                                              Log out user

LOGOUT

---

Forces the current user to be logged out and waits to log in a new user.

---

## RETRY                          Return control to calling program

RETRY

---

Returns control to the command line of the calling program. The command line is re-executed. This differs from the RETURN command which gives control to the next command line in the calling program.

This command is used when errors are encountered and must be repeated until they are completed.

## SET ENCRYPTION ON | OFF     Encrypt data

SET ENCRYPTION ON | OFF

ON specifies that files made by the COPY, JOIN or TOTAL commands are to be encrypted.

OFF specifies that files created this way are not to be encrypted.

Default is ON.

Note: SET ENCRYPTION OFF must be specified if you use the COPY command with any of the following clauses: DELIMITED, DIF, PFS, SDF, SYLK, or WKS.

## SET EXCLUSIVE ON | OFF
### Specify database sharing

SET EXCLUSIVE ON | OFF

ON specifies that any database that is subsequently opened is accessible only by the current user. These databases are not shareable.

OFF specifies that any database that is subsequently opened is shareable.

Default is ON.

--> USE EXCLUSIVE

114

---

**SET PRINTER**                          Send to network printer
(IBM PC Network)

```
SET PRINTER TO \\<computer name>\<printer name> =
                <destination>
```

Redirects printer output from <destination> to the network printer <printer name> attached to server <computer name> in an IBM PC Network.

<computer name> is the server identifier

<printer name> is the printer identifier

<destination> is the standard device identifier (LPT1, LPT2 or LPT3)

**SET PRINTER**                          Send to network printer
(Novell/86 Network)

```
SET PRINTER TO \\ SPOOLER
```

Redirects printer output to the network printer in a Novell/86 Network.

---

## SET PRINTER — Send to local printer

```
SET PRINTER TO <device>
```

Sends output to the DOS <device>.

<device> can be one of the following:

> COM1
> COM2
> LPT1
> LPT2
> LPT3
> PRN

## UNLOCK — Release locks

```
UNLOCK [ALL]
```

Removes the lock for the record or database in the current work area.

ALL removes all locks in all work areas.

## USE EXCLUSIVE — Open database exclusively

```
USE     [<filename>] [INDEX <index list>]
        EXCLUSIVE [ALIAS <alias name>]
```

Opens the database <filename> in the current work area. If the INDEX <index list> clause is included, the specified index files are also.

ALIAS <alias name> assigns an alias name to the current work area.

116

EXCLUSIVE opens the database as non-shareable. If any of the following commands are used, the database must be opened as EXCLUSIVE:

> INSERT
> MODIFY STRUCTURE
> PACK
> REINDEX
> ZAP

USE without parameters closes the current in USE database and any associated index files.

```
--> SET EXCLUSIVE
```

# Appendix A

## OPERATORS

dBASE III Plus supports four types of operators: comparison, mathematical, logical and string operators.

### Comparison operators

Comparisons have logical results: .T. = true or .F. = false. Comparison operators can be used to compare character, numeric, and date expressions. Both expressions to be compared must be of the same type.

| < | less than |
|---|---|
| > | greater than |
| = | equal |
| <> or # | not equal |
| <= | less than or equal |
| >= | greater than or equal |
| $ | substring comparison. Searches a string for a substring. A comparison is .T. (true) if the left expression is identical to the right expression or contained within it; otherwise it is false. |

### Mathematical operators

Mathematical operators perform mathmatical computations and produce numeric results.

| + | addition |
|---|---|
| - | subtraction |
| * | multiplication |
| / | division |
| ** or ^ | exponentiation |
| () | change order of processing |

## Logical operators

Logical operators compare logical expressions. The result is also a logical expression.

| | |
|---|---|
| .AND. | logical AND |
| .OR. | logical OR |
| .NOT. | logical NOT, also operates on a single expression |

## String operators

+         Concatenation operator, concatenates multiple strings into one

-         Concatenation operator, concatenates multiple strings into one. Trailing blank spaces are moved to the end of the concatenated string.

## Precedence of the operators

Comparison and string operators are always evaluated from left to right.

Mathematical operators are evaluated in the following order (highest to lowest):

> 1. ** or ^
> 2. * and /
> 3. + and -

Logical operators are evaluated in the following order (highest to lowest):

> 1. .NOT.
> 2. .AND.
> 3. .OR.

Different operator types within an expression are evaluated in the
following order (highest to lowest):

      1. Mathematical and string operators
      2. Comparsion operators
      3. Logical operators

# Appendix B

## Fields, variables, and expressions

### Fields

Field names can contain up to 10 characters A field name must begin with a letter and may not contain any imbedded blanks.

The following field types are available:

| | |
|---|---|
| C | character fields |
| D | date fields |
| L | logical fields |
| N | numeric fields |
| M | memo fields |

Character fields can contain all printable characters and may be up to 254 characters long.

Date fields are always eight bytes long. A date can be added to a numeric value. A date can be subtracted from another date and a numeric value can be subtracted from a date.

Logical fields occupy one byte. The entries T, t, Y, and y are allowed for logical .T. = true and F, f, N, and n for logical .F. = false.

The length of a numeric fields corresponds to the number of digits entered in the field. The sign and decimal point each occupy one decimal position. Numeric operators are accurate to 15.9 digits.

Memo fields are passages of text which are stored in an associated text database with the extension .DBT. A memo field occupies 10 bytes in a database record. The memo text itself can be 5000 bytes long when the dBase III Plus text editor is used, or longer if another text editor is used (specified using the WP parameter in the CONFIG.DB file).

## Variables

Variable names can contain up to 10 characters. A variable name must begin with a letter and can contain alphabetic, numeric and underline characters.

Normally a maximum of 256 variables of types character, date, numerical, and logical with a total length of 6000 bytes can be active and one time. The limit of 6000 bytes can be varied by changing the MVARSIZ parameter in the CONFIG.DB file, if that amount of memory is available.

If a field name and variable name are identical the field name is used for all operations. You can explicitty refer to the variable name by prefixing the variable name with M→.

The properties of variable types correspond to those of the field types.

## Expressions

A dBase expression can consist of one or more of the following terms:

- fields
- variables
- constants
- functions
- operators

Within an expression, the terms must be of the same data type (character, data, logical or numeric).

# Appendix C

## Data file formats

### Catalog files (.CAT)

Contains all dBase files which are assigned to a given application, for example. All catalog files are themselves managed in the main catalog "CATALOG.CAT". Catalog files are activated with the command SET CATALOG.

### Database files (.DBF)

Database files contain the data, organized in up to 1 billion records with up to 128 fields. Each record can contain up to 4000 bytes. Databases are created with CREATE. Their structure can be changed with MODIFY STRUCTURE.

### Memo files (.DBT)

Memo files are assigned to a database to hold the contents of a defined memo field. The contents of all memo fields of one database are stored in a single memo file. Each record can contain up to 128 memo fields. When using the built in dBase editor each memo field can contain up to 5000 characters, or more if another editor is used (specified by the UP parameter in the CONFIG.DB file). At least 512 bytes are used per memo field and record. Memo files are created automatically at the same time as a database file.

### Index files (.NDX)

Index files order database in a logical sequence (alphabetical, chronological, or numerical). The physical order of the records in a database is not changed. The index file contains the value of the key field and the corresponding record number. If a database and an associated index file is USEd, it is accessed in indexed order. An index can be created with the INDEX command.

## Command and procedure files (.PRG)

Command and procedure files are stored in ASCII format and can be edited with any built in text editor. The command MODIFY COMMAND uses the built in dBase editor or the text editor specified by the TEDIT parameter in the CONFIG.DB file.

## Format files (.FMT)

Format files contain a sequence of @...SAY | GET commands and create individual masks for the data input and output. These ASCII files can be edited with any editor.

They can also be created from screen files.

## Label files (.LBL)

Label files contain the specifications and parameters for creating individual labels. These created or changed with CREATE LABEL or MODIFY LABEL commands.

## Variable files (.MEM)

Variable files store up to 256 variables. They are created by the SAVE command. The stored variables can be loaded and activated again with the RESTORE command.

## Query files (.QRY)

Query files contain filter conditions for the open database. They are created or changed with CREATE QUERY or MODIFY QUERY and activated with the SET FILTER TO command.

## Screen files (.SCR)

Screen files contain data which can be used for creating and/or editing format files. They can be created or changed with CREATE SCREEN or MODIFY SCREEN commands.

## View files (.VUE)

View files store a work environment: databases, index and format files, a field list, filter conditions, relations, and so on. They are created or changed with CREATE VIEW, MODIFY VIEW or CREATE VIEW FROM ENVIRONMENT commands.

## Report form files (.FRM)

Report form files contain the data for creating a report with the help of the REPORT command. They are created or edited with the CREATE REPORT or MODIFY REPORT command.

## Text files (.TXT)

Text files are used for import and export of data to and from foreign programs (such as with the APPEND FROM and COPY commands). These are standard ASCII files which contain only printable characters. The SET ALTERNATE commands also creates a text file.

# Appendix D

## Configuration file - CONFIG.DB

This standard ASCII file contains the configuration parameters, which are automatically activated when dBase III Plus is started. If the CONFIG.DB file is not present, the default values are used.

Each parameter assignment has the form <keyword> = <value>.

Many of these keywords perform the same function as the corresponding SET command.

| Keyword | Possible Value |
|---------|----------------|
| ALTERNATE | <filename> |
| BELL | ON \| OFF |
| BUCKET | 1 to 31<br>Amount of memory for the PICTURE and RANGE commands (in K bytes). Default is 2. |
| CARRY | ON \| OFF |
| CATALOG | <filename> |
| CENTURY | ON \| OFF |
| COLOR | <color option list> |
| COMMAND | <command>[command arguments]<br><command> is a dBase command (such as ASSIST) and is automatically executed on startup. |
| CONFIRM | ON \| OFF |
| CONSOLE | ON \| OFF |
| DEBUG | ON \| OFF |
| DECIMALS | 0 to 14 |
| DEFAULT | <drive> |

127

| DELETED | ON \| OFF |
|---------|-----------|
| DELIMITER | ON \| OFF |
| DELIMITER | one or two characters |
| DEVICE | SCREEN \| PRINTER |
| ECHO | ON \| OFF |
| ESCAPE | ON \| OFF |
| EXACT | ON \| OFF |
| F (2-9) | <command list> assigns one or more dBase commands to the function keys 2 thru 9. |
| GETS | 35 to 1023 |
| HEADING | ON \| OFF |
| HELP | ON \| OFF |
| HISTORY | 0 to 16000 |
| INTENSITY | ON \| OFF |
| MARGIN | 1 to 254 |
| MAXMEM | 256 to 720 Amount of memory which dBase III Plus makes available when another program is executed (in K bytes). Default is 256K. |
| MEMOWIDTH | 8 to maximum memory |
| MENU | ON \| OFF |
| MVARSIZ | 1 to 31 Amount of memory reserved for memory variables (in K bytes). |
| PATH | <pathname> |
| PRINT | ON \| OFF |
| PROMPT | <string> |
| SAFETY | ON \| OFF |
| SCOREBOARD | ON \| OFF |
| STATUS | ON \| OFF |
| STEP | ON \| OFF |
| TALK | ON \| OFF |

| TEDIT | <program name> The name of the text editor to be used for CREATE or MODIFY command. |
|-------|------------------------------------------------------------------------------------|
| TYPEAHEAD | 0 to 32000 |
| UNIQUE | ON \| OFF |
| VIEW | <filename> |
| WP | <program name> The name of the program that will be executed when editing memo fields. |

# Appendix E

## Error Codes

| | |
|----|----|
| 1 | File does not exist |
| 2 | Unassigned file no |
| 3 | File is already open |
| 4 | End of file encountered |
| 5 | Record is out of range |
| 6 | Too many files are open |
| 7 | File already exists |
| 8 | Unbalanced parenthsis |
| 9 | Data type mismatch |
| 10 | Syntax error |
| 11 | Invalid function argument |
| 12 | Variable not found |
| 13 | ALIAS not found |
| 15 | Not a dBase database |
| 16 | Unrecognized command verb |
| 17 | Cannot select requested database |
| 18 | Line exceeds maximum of 254 characters |
| 19 | Index file does not match database |
| 20 | Record is not in index |
| 21 | Out of memory variable memory |
| 22 | Out of memory variable slots |
| 23 | Index is too big (100 char maximum) |
| 24 | ALIAS name already in use |
| 26 | Database is not indexed |
| 27 | Not a numeric expression |
| 28 | Too many indices |
| 29 | File is not accessible |
| 30 | Position is off the screen |
| 31 | Invalid function name |
| 33 | Structure invalid |
| 34 | Operation with Memo field invalid |
| 35 | Unterminated string |

| 36 | Unrecognized phrase/keywork in command |
|----|----------------------------------------|
| 37 | Not a Logical expression |
| 38 | Beginning of file encountered |
| 39 | Numeric overflow (data was lost) |
| 41 | .DBT file cannot be opened |
| 42 | CONTINUE without LOCATE |
| 43 | Insufficient memory |
| 44 | Cyclic relation |
| 45 | Not a character expression |
| 46 | Illegal value |
| 47 | No fields to process |
| 53 | There are no files of the type requested in this drive or catalog |
| 54 | Label file invalid |
| 55 | Memory Variable file is invalid |
| 57 | Execution error on CHR(): Out of range |
| 58 | Execution error on LOG(): Zero or negative |
| 59 | Execution error on SPACE(): Too large |
| 60 | Execution error on SPACE(): negative |
| 61 | Execution error on SQRT(): negative |
| 62 | Execution errror on SUBSTR(): Start point out of range |
| 63 | Execution error on STR(): Out of range |
| 76 | Execution error on -: Concatenated string too large |
| 77 | Execution error on +: Concatenated string too large |
| 78 | Execution error on ^ or **: Negative base, fractional exponent |
| 79 | Execution error STORE: String too large |
| 87 | Execution error on NDX(): Invalid index number |
| 88 | Execution eror on REPLICATE(): String too large |

| 90  | Operation with Logical field invalid |
| --- | --- |
| 91  | File was not LOADed |
| 92  | Unable to load COMMAND.COM |
| 93  | No PARAMETER statement found |
| 94  | Wrong number of parameters |
| 95  | Valid only in programs |
| 96  | Mismatched DO WHILE and    ENDDO |
| 101 | Not suspended |
| 102 | Exectution error on STUFF(): String too large |
| 103 | DOs nested too deep. |
| 104 | Unknown function key |
| 105 | Table is full |
| 106 | Invalid index number |
| 107 | Invalid operator |
| 109 | Record is in use by another |
| 111 | Cannot write to read-only file |
| 112 | Index expression is too big (220 char maximum). |
| 115 | Invalid DIF File Header |
| 116 | Invalid DIF vector - DBF field mismatch |
| 117 | Invalid DIF Type Indicator |
| 118 | Invalid DIF Character |
| 119 | Invalid SYLK File Header |
| 120 | Invalid SYLK File Dimension Bounds |
| 121 | Invalid SYLK File Format |
| 122 | Data Catlog has not been established |
| 123 | Invalid printer port |
| 124 | Invalid printer redirection |
| 126 | Printer is either not connected or turned off |
| 127 | Not a valid VIEW file |
| 131 | Database is encrypted |
| 134 | Not a valid QUERY file |
| 136 | Unsupported path given |
| 138 | No fields were found to copy |

| 139 | Cannot JOIN a file with itself |
| 140 | Not a valid PFS file |
| 141 | Fields list too complicated |
| 142 | Relation record is in use by others |
| 143 | Query not valid for this environment |
| 146 | Maximum path length exceeded |
| 147 | Cannot append in column order |
| 148 | Network server busy |
| 149 | Master catalog is empty |

# Quick Index

| | |
|---|---|
| ! | 7 |
| & | 82 |
| * | 7 |
| ? | 7 |
| ?? | 8 |
| @...SAY | 8-10 |
| @...TO | 10 |
| @...CLEAR | 8 |
| @...GET | 8-10,48 |
| ABS | 82 |
| ACCEPT | 10 |
| APPEND | 10-11 |
| APPEND FROM | 11 |
| ASC | 83 |
| ASSIST | 12 |
| AT | 83 |
| AVERAGE | 12 |
| BOF | 84 |
| BROWSE | 12 |
| CALL | 13 |
| CANCEL | 14 |
| CDOW | 84 |
| CHANGE | 14,111 |
| CHR | 84 |
| CLEAR | 14 |
| CLEAR FIELDS | 15 |
| CLEAR GETS | 15 |
| CLEAR MEMORY | 15 |
| CLEAR TYPEAHEAD | 15 |
| CLOSE | 16 |

| | |
|---|---|
| CMONTH | 85 |
| COL | 85 |
| CONTINUE | 16 |
| COPY FILE | 17 |
| COPY STRUCTURE | 17 |
| COPY STRUCTURE EXTENDED | 18 |
| COPY TO | 18 |
| COUNT | 19 |
| CREATE | 20 |
| CREATE FROM | 20 |
| CREATE LABEL | 20 |
| CREATE QUERY | 21 |
| CREATE REPORT | 22 |
| CREATE SCREEN | 23 |
| CREATE VIEW | 23 |
| CREATE VIEW FROM ENV | 24 |
| CTOD | 85 |
| DATE() | 86 |
| DAY | 86 |
| DBF | 86 |
| DELETE | 24 |
| DELETED | 87 |
| DIR | 25 |
| DISKSPACE | 87 |
| DISPLAY | 25 |
| DISPLAY HISTORY | 26 |
| DISPLAY MEMORY | 26 |
| DISPLAY STATUS | 26,112 |
| DISPLAY STRUCTURE | 27 |
| DISPLAY USERS | 112 |
| DO | 27 |
| DO CASE | 28 |
| DOW() | 87 |
| DTOC | 88 |
| EDIT | 29 |
| EJECT | 29 |
| EOF | 88 |
| ERASE | 29 |
| ERROR | 88 |

| | |
|---|---|
| EXIT | 30 |
| EXP | 89 |
| EXPORT | 30 |
| FIELD | 89 |
| FILE | 89 |
| FIND | 30 |
| FKLABEL | 90 |
| FKMAX | 90 |
| FOUND | 90 |
| GETENV | 91 |
| GO \| GOTO | 31 |
| HELP | 31 |
| IF | 32 |
| IIF | 91 |
| IMPORT | 32 |
| INDEX | 33 |
| INKEY | 91-92 |
| INPUT | 34 |
| INSERT | 34 |
| INT | 92 |
| ISALPHA | 93 |
| ISCOLOR | 93 |
| ISLOWER | 93 |
| ISUPPER | 94 |
| JOIN | 35 |
| LABEL FORM | 36 |
| LEFT | 94 |
| LEN | 95 |
| LIST | 36 |
| LIST HISTORY | 37 |
| LIST MEMORY | 37 |
| LIST STATUS | 38,112-113 |
| LIST STRUCTURE | 38 |
| LOAD | 39 |
| LOCATE | 39 |
| LOCK | 13 |
| LOG | 95 |
| LOGOUT | 113 |
| LOOP | 39 |

| | |
|---|---|
| LOWER | 95 |
| LTRIM | 96 |
| LUPDATE | 96 |
| MAX | 96 |
| MESSAGE | 97 |
| MIN | 97 |
| MOD | 97 |
| MODIFY | 23,43 |
| MODIFY COMMAND | 40 |
| MODIFY LABEL | 40 |
| MODIFY QUERY | 41 |
| MODIFY REPORT | 42 |
| MODIFY SCREEN | 42 |
| MODIFY STRUCTURE | 43 |
| MODIFY VIEW | 43 |
| MONTH | 98 |
| NDX | 98 |
| NOTE | 44 |
| ON ERROR | 44 |
| ON ESCAPE | 45 |
| ON KEY | 45 |
| OS | 98 |
| PACK | 45 |
| PARAMETERS | 46 |
| PCOL | 99 |
| PRIVATE | 46 |
| PROCEDURE | 47 |
| PROW | 99 |
| PUBLIC | 47 |
| QUIT | 47 |
| READ | 48 |
| READKEY | 99-100 |
| RECALL | 48 |
| RECCOUNT | 101 |
| RECNO | 101 |
| RECSIZE | 102 |
| REINDEX | 48 |
| RELEASE | 49 |
| RENAME | 49 |

| | |
|---|---|
| REPLACE | 49 |
| REPLICATE | 102 |
| REPORT | 50 |
| RESTORE | 51 |
| RESUME | 51 |
| RETRY | 51 |
| RETRY | 113 |
| RETURN | 52 |
| RIGHT | 103 |
| ROUND | 103 |
| ROW | 104 |
| RTRIM | 104 |
| RUN | 52 |
| SAVE | 52 |
| SEEK | 53 |
| SELECT | 53 |
| SET | 53 |
| SET ALTERNATE ON \| OFF | 54 |
| SET ALTERNATE TO | 54 |
| SET BELL ON \| OFF | 54 |
| SET CARRY ON \| OFF | 55 |
| SET CATALOG ON\| OFF | 55 |
| SET CATALOG TO | 55 |
| SET CENTURY ON \| OFF | 56 |
| SET COLOR ON \| OFF | 56 |
| SET COLOR TO | 56 |
| SET CONFIRM ON \| OFF | 58 |
| SET CONSOLE ON \| OFF | 58 |
| SET DATE | 58 |
| SET DEBUG ON \| OFF | 59 |
| SET DECIMALS TO | 59 |
| SET DEFAULT TO | 59 |
| SET DELETED ON \| OFF | 60 |
| SET DELIMITERS ON \| OFF | 60 |
| SET DELIMITERS TO | 61 |
| SET DEVICE TO | 61 |
| SET DOHISTORY ON \| OFF | 61 |
| SET ECHO ON \| OFF | 61 |
| SET ENCRYPTION ON \| OFF | 62 |
| | 114 |

SET ESCAPE ON | OFF                                        62
SET EXACT ON | OFF                                         63
SET EXCLUSIVE ON | OFF                                    114
SET FIELDS ON | OFF                                        63
SET FIELDS TO                                              63
SET FILTER TO                                              64
SET FIXED ON | OFF                                         65
SET FORMAT TO                                              65
SET FUNCTION TO                                            65
SET HEADING ON | OFF                                       66
SET HISTORY ON | OFF                                       66
SET HISTORY TO                                             67
SET INDEX TO                                               67
SET INTENSITY ON | OFF                                     68
SET MARGIN TO                                              68
SET MEMOWIDTH TO                                           69
SET MENU ON | OFF                                          69
SET MESSAGE TO                                             69
SET ODOMETER TO                                            70
SET ORDER TO                                               70
SET PATH TO                                                71
SET PRINT ON | OFF                                         71
SET PRINTER                                          115-116
SET PRINTER TO                                          71-72
SET PROCEDURE TO                                           72
SET RELATION TO                                            72
SET SAFETY ON | OFF                                        73
SET SCOREBOARD ON | OFF                                    73
SET STATUS ON | OFF                                        74
SET STEP ON | OFF                                          74
SET TALK ON | OFF                                          74
SET TITLE ON | OFF                                         75
SET TYPEAHEAD TO                                           75
SET UNIQUE ON | OFF                                        75
SET VIEW TO                                                76
SKIP                                                       76
SORT                                                       77
SPACE                                                     104
SQRT                                                      105

| | |
|---|---:|
| STORE | 77 |
| STR | 105 |
| STUFF | 105 |
| SUBSTR | 106 |
| SUM | 78 |
| SUSPEND | 78 |
| TEXT | 79 |
| TIME | 106 |
| TOTAL | 79 |
| TRANSFORM | 107 |
| TRIM | 108 |
| TYPE | 80,109 |
| UNLOCK | 116 |
| UPDATE | 80 |
| UPPER | 110 |
| USE | 81 |
| USE EXCLUSIVE | 116 |
| VAL | 110 |
| VERSION | 110 |
| WAIT | 81 |
| YEAR | 110 |
| ZAP | 81 |

# Subject Index

*This index lists dBase's command set by general subject, the command/function descriptions grouped within the subject heading, and the commands/functions themselves to the right of the descriptions:*

## Controlling peripherals

| | | |
|---|---|---|
| Clear input buffer | CLEAR TYPEAHEAD | 15 |
| Clear screen | CLEAR | 14 |
| Display SET parameter menu | SET | 53 |
| Send printer formfeed | EJECT | 29 |

## Converting characters

| | | |
|---|---|---|
| Convert ASCII code to character | CHR | 84 |
| Convert character to ACSII code | ASC | 83 |
| Convert date variable to string | DTOC | 88 |
| Convert numeric variable to string | STR | 105 |
| Convert string to date variable | CTOD | 85 |
| Convert string to numeric variable | VAL | 110 |

## Creating application programs

| | | |
|---|---|---|
| Accept parameters | PARAMETERS | 46 |
| Deactivate GET commands | CLEAR GETS | 15 |
| Declare local variables | PRIVATE | 46 |
| Define global variables | PUBLIC | 47 |
| Define routine in procedure | PROCEDURE | 47 |
| Display block of text | TEXT | 79 |
| End DO WHILE command | EXIT | 30 |
| End the application program | CANCEL | 14 |
| Execute alternative commands | DO CASE | 28 |
| Execute application program | DO | 27 |
| Execute conditional command | IF | 32 |
| Insert comment line | NOTE | 44 |
| Leave dBase | QUIT | 47 |
| Return control to calling program | RETRY | 51 |

141

| | | |
|---|---|---|
| Return control to calling program | RETURN | 52 |
| Return day of the week | DOW | 87 |
| Set error trap | ON ERROR | 44 |
| Set ESC key trap | ON ESCAPE | 45 |
| Set keypress trap | ON KEY | 45 |
| Substitute macro | & | 82 |

## Creating and modifying a database

| | | |
|---|---|---|
| Change database structure | MODIFY STRUCTURE | 43 |
| Combine two database files | JOIN | 35 |
| Copy .DBF structure | COPY STRUCTURE EXTENDED | 18 |
| Copy database records | COPY TO | 18 |
| Create database | CREATE | 20 |
| Create database from structure file | CREATE FROM | 20 |
| Create format file | CREATE SCREEN | 23 |
| Create index file | INDEX | 33 |
| Create mask file | MODIFY SCREEN | 42 |
| Create query file | CREATE QUERY | 21 |
| Create query file | MODIFY QUERY | 41 |
| Create report file | CREATE REPORT | 22 |
| Create report file | MODIFY REPORT | 42 |
| Create sorted copy of database | SORT | 77 |
| Create totals file | TOTAL | 79 |
| Create view file | CREATE VIEW | 23 |
| Define label file | CREATE LABEL | 20 |
| Define label file | MODIFY LABEL | 40 |
| Define work environment | CREATE VIEW | 23 |
| Copy .DBF file to PFS format | EXPORT | 30 |
| Duplicate database structure | COPY STRUCTURE | 17 |
| Duplicate file | COPY FILE | 17 |
| Make .DBF file from a PFS file | IMPORT | 32 |
| Modify command file | MODIFY COMMAND | 40 |
| Save current memory variables | SAVE | 52 |

# Date and time

Convert date to day of week        CDOW              84
Convert date to month              CMONTH            85
Return day of the week             DOW               87
Return system date                 DATE              86
Return system time                 TIME              106
Return the month                   MONTH             98
Return year                        YEAR              110

# Debug/command trace

Continue program execution         RESUME            51
Display history buffer             DISPLAY HISTORY   26
Halt program execution             SUSPEND           78
List history buffer                LIST HISTORY      37

# Determining parameters

Beginning of file?                 BOF               84
Does file exists?                  FILE              89
End of file?                       EOF               88
Environment variable from DOS      GETENV            91
Function key assignment            FKLABEL           90
Immediate IF                       IIF               91
Is first character alphabetic?     ISALPHA           93
Is first character lowercase?      ISLOWER           93
Is first character uppercase?      ISUPPER           94
Is screen display color mode?      ISCOLOR           93
Mark record for deletion           DELETE            24
Number of function keys            FKMAX             90
Operating system name              OS                98
Result of search operation         FOUND             90
Return ASCII code of last key
pressed                            INKEY             91
Return column number of cursor     COL               85
Return current record number       RECNO             101
Return data type                   TYPE              109

| | | |
|---|---|---|
| Return error code | ERROR | 88 |
| Return error message | MESSAGE | 97 |
| Return fieldname | FIELD | 89 |
| Return key code | READKEY | 99 |
| Return length of string | LEN | 95 |
| Return line number of cursor | ROW | 104 |
| Return number of records in database | RECCOUNT | 101 |
| Return printer column position | PCOL | 99 |
| Return printer line position | PROW | 99 |
| Return record length | RECSIZE | 102 |

## Displaying the data

| | | |
|---|---|---|
| Calculate arithmetic mean | AVERAGE | 12 |
| Count number of records | COUNT | 19 |
| Create report from REPORT file | REPORT | 50 |
| Creates labels from label file | LABEL FORM | 36 |
| Delete field list | CLEAR FIELDS | 15 |
| Display border | @...TO | 10 |
| Display expression | ?? | 8 |
| Display records | DISPLAY | 25 |
| Display/input formatted data | @...SAY | 8 |
| List records in database | LIST | 36 |
| Sum the values of numeric fields | SUM | 78 |

## Executing foreign programs

| | | |
|---|---|---|
| Execute DOS command | RUN | 52 |
| Execute machine language program | CALL | 13 |
| Load machine language program | LOAD | 39 |

## Getting help/and status information

| | | |
|---|---|---|
| Activate dBase HELP menus | HELP | 31 |
| Display ASCII files | TYPE | 80,109 |
| Display database info | DISPLAY STRUCTURE | 27 |
| Display directory | DIR | 25 |
| Display menu mode | ASSIST | 12 |
| Display status information | DISPLAY STATUS | 26 |

| | | |
|---|---|---|
| Display variables | DISPLAY MEMORY | 26 |
| List database structure | LIST STRUCTURE | 38 |
| List status information | LIST STATUS | 38 |

## Inserting data into a database

| | | |
|---|---|---|
| Append new record to database | APPEND | 10 |
| Edit/append records | BROWSE | 12 |
| Insert record in database | INSERT | 34 |

## Mathematical functions

| | | |
|---|---|---|
| Return absolute value | ABS | 82 |
| Return exponentiation function | EXP | 89 |
| Return integer | INT | 92 |
| Return larger of two values | MAX | 96 |
| Return natural logarithm | LOG | 95 |
| Return remainder of division | MOD | 97 |
| Return smaller of two values | MIN | 97 |
| Return square root | SQRT | 105 |
| Round numeric value | ROUND | 103 |

## Moving the record pointer

| | | |
|---|---|---|
| Move record pointer forward or backward | SKIP | 76 |
| Position record pointer | GO \| GOTO | 31 |
| Resume search | CONTINUE | 16 |
| Search current database | LOCATE | 39 |
| Search indexed database | FIND | 30 |
| Search indexed database | SEEK | 53 |

## Processing characters

| | | |
|---|---|---|
| Convert lower to uppercase | UPPER | 109 |
| Convert to PICTURE format | TRANSFORM | 107 |
| Convert upper to lowercase | LOWER | 95 |
| Copies a string n times | REPLICATE | 102 |
| Extract leftmost characters | LEFT | 94 |
| Extract rightmost characters | RIGHT | 103 |
| Extract substring | SUBSTR | 106 |
| Find starting position of substring | AT | 83 |
| Remove leading blanks | LTRIM | 96 |

| Remove trailing blanks | RTRIM | 104 |
| Remove trailing blanks | TRIM | 108 |
| Replace characters in string | STUFF | 105 |
| Return string of blanks | SPACE | 104 |

## Processing data

| Activates @..GET commands | READ | 48 |
| Change contents of selected fields | REPLACE | 49 |
| Edit records | EDIT | 29 |
| Edit selected fields and records | CHANGE | 14 |
| Mark record for deletion | DELETE | 24 |
| Remove deletion mark | RECALL | 48 |
| Remove records marked or deletion | PACK | 45 |
| Update from another database | UPDATE | 80 |

## Processing the database

| Change filename | RENAME | 49 |
| Clear screen | CLEAR | 14 |
| Close dBase files | CLOSE | 16 |
| Copies records into database | APPEND FROM | 11 |
| Delete all records | ZAP | 80 |
| Delete file from directory | ERASE | 29 |
| Open database | USE | 80 |
| Rebuild index file | REINDEX | 48 |
| Select work area | SELECT | 53 |

## Processing variables

| Assign value to variable | STORE | 77 |
| Delete variables | RELEASE | 49 |
| Input data from keyboard | ACCEPT | 10 |
| Input data from keyboard | INPUT | 34 |
| Interrupt processing | WAIT | 81 |
| List variables | LIST MEMORY | 37 |
| Read variable file | RESTORE | 51 |
| Release memory variables | CLEAR MEMORY | 15 |

# The SET commands

| | | |
|---|---|---|
| Activate catalog | SET CATALOG ON\| OFF | 55 |
| Allow unique keys | SET UNIQUE ON \| OFF | 75 |
| Assign function keys | SET FUNCTION TO | 65-66 |
| Change field delimiter | SET DELIMITERS TO | 61 |
| Change index | SET ORDER TO | 70 |
| Change memo width display | SET MEMOWIDTH TO | 69 |
| Confirm end of field | SET CONFIRM ON \| OFF | 58 |
| Confirm warnings | SET SAFETY ON \| OFF | 73 |
| Connect databases | SET RELATION TO | 72-73 |
| Copy data from previous record | SET CARRY ON \| OFF | 55 |
| Define field list | SET FIELDS TO | 64 |
| Display century | SET CENTURY ON \| OFF | 56 |
| Display column heading | SET HEADING ON \| OFF | 66 |
| Display command result | SET TALK ON \| OFF | 74 |
| Display commands | SET ECHO ON \| OFF | 59,62 |
| Display cursor menu | SET MENU ON \| OFF | 69 |
| Display field delimiter | SET DELIMITERS ON \| OFF | 60 |
| Display inverse fields | SET INTENSITY ON \| OFF | 68 |
| Display status line | SET STATUS ON \| OFF | 74 |
| Display status messages | SET SCOREBOARD | 73 |
| Display user message | SET MESSAGE TO | 69 |
| Enable color monitor | SET COLOR ON \| OFF | 56 |

| | | |
|---|---|---|
| Enable ESC key | SET ESCAPE ON \| OFF | 62 |
| Enable exact comparison | SET EXACT ON \| OFF | 63 |
| Enable field protection | SET FIELDS ON \| OFF | 15,63 |
| Encrypt data | SET ENCRYPTION ON \| OFF | 114 |
| Hide deleted records | SET DELETED ON \| OFF | 60 |
| Open index files | SET INDEX TO | 67 |
| Open procedure file | SET PROCEDURE TO | 71 |
| Open redirection file | SET ALTERNATE TO | 54 |
| Open view file | SET VIEW TO | 76 |
| Opens a CATALOG file | SET CATALOG TO | 55 |
| Opens format file | SET FORMAT TO | 65 |
| Prompt for title | SET TITLE ON \| OFF | 75 |
| Record commands | SET HISTORY ON \| OFF | 67 |
| Record program commands | SET DOHISTORY ON \| OFF | 61 |
| Redirect screen output | SET ALTERNATE ON \| OFF | 54 |
| Screen display on/off | SET CONSOLE ON \| OFF | 58 |
| Select color and screen attributes | SET COLOR TO | 56 |
| Send ECHO output to printer | SET DEBUG ON \| OFF | 59 |
| Send output to printer | SET PRINT ON \| OFF | 71 |
| Send to network printer | SET PRINTER | 115-116 |
| Set date format | SET DATE | 58-59 |
| Set default drive | SET DEFAULT TO | 59 |
| Set left printer margin | SET MARGIN TO | 68 |
| Set number of decimal places | SET DECIMALS TO | 59 |
| Set number of decimal places | SET FIXED ON \| OFF | 65 |
| Set output device | SET DEVICE TO | 61 |
| Set single-step mode | SET STEP ON \| OFF | 74 |

| | | |
|---|---|---|
| Set size of input buffer | SET TYPEAHEAD TO | 75 |
| Specify database sharing | SET EXCLUSIVE ON \| OFF | 114 |
| Specify filter condition | SET FILTER TO | 64 |
| Specify number of commands | SET HISTORY TO | 67 |
| Specify printer port | SET PRINTER TO | 70 |
| Specify search path | SET PATH TO | 70 |
| Turn bell on or off | SET BELL ON \| OFF | 54 |

# Index

| | | | |
|---|---|---|---|
| ! (execute DOS command) | 7 | BEFORE | 34 |
| & (substitute macro) | 82 | beginning of file | 84 |
| * (insert commentary) | 7 | bell | 54 |
| ? (display expression) | 7 | BLANK | 10,34 |
| ?? (display expression) | 8 | BOF | 84 |
| @...CLEAR | 8 | BROWSE | 12 |
| @...GET | 8-10,15,48 | | |
| @...SAY | 8-10 | CALL | 13 |
| @...TO | 10 | CANCEL | 14 |
| | | .CAT | 124 |
| .AND. | 120 | catalog files | 55,124 |
| ABS | 82 | CDOW | 84 |
| absolute value | 82 | century display | 56 |
| ACCEPT | 10 | CHANGE | 14,111 |
| add records | 10,12 | change field contents | 50 |
| ADDITIVE | 51 | change filename | 50 |
| ADMINISTRATOR | 110 | change index | 70 |
| ALL | 16 | character code | 83,84 |
| ALL EXCEPT | 46 | character fields | 122 |
| ALL LIKE | 46 | CHR | 84 |
| ALTERNATE | 16 | @...CLEAR | 8 |
| APPEND | 10-11 | CLEAR | 14 |
| APPEND FROM | 11 | CLEAR ALL | 15 |
| append record | 10,12-13 | CLEAR FIELDS | 15 |
| application program | 27 | CLEAR GETS | 15 |
| arithmetic mean | 12 | CLEAR MEMORY | 15 |
| ASC | 83 | CLEAR TYPEAHEAD | 15 |
| ASCII | 80,83,91 | clear input buffer | 15 |
| ASSIST | 12 | clear screen | 8,14 |
| AT | 83 | CLOSE | 16 |
| AVERAGE | 12 | close file | 16 |
| | | CMONTH | 85 |
| | | COL | 85 |

| | | | |
|---|---|---|---|
| color | 56-57,93 | CTOD | 85 |
| column heading | 66 | cursor | 85 |
| COLUMNS | 22 | | |
| combine files | 35 | data encryption | 114 |
| command file | 40,125 | data file formats | 124-126 |
| COMMAND.COM | 7 | data input | 10,34 |
| commands | 7-81 | database files | 124 |
| comments | 7,44 | database information | 27 |
| comparison operators | 119 | DATABASES | 16 |
| COMSPEC | 7 | DATE | 86 |
| conditional commands | 32 | date commands | 58,84-86 |
| CONFIG.DB | 40,123,127 | date fields | 121 |
| configuration | 127-129 | DAY | 86 |
| CONNECT | 21,41 | .DBF | 11,31 |
| CONTINUE | 16 | DBF | 86 |
| continue program | 51 | decimal places | 59,65 |
| COPY FILE | 17 | default drive | 59 |
| COPY STRUC. EXT. | 18 | define field list | 63-64 |
| COPY STRUCTURE | 17 | define label file | 20-21,40-41 |
| COPY TO | 18 | define routine | 47 |
| copy files | 31,33 | DELETE | 24 |
| copy records | 11,18 | delete field | 15 |
| COUNT | 19 | delete file | 30 |
| count records | 19 | delete record | 24,45,81 |
| CREATE | 6,20 | delete variable | 49 |
| CREATE FROM | 20 | DELETED | 87 |
| CREATE LABEL | 20 | DELIMITED | 11 |
| CREATE QUERY | 21 | DELIMITED WITH | |
| CREATE REPORT | 22 | BLANK | 11,19 |
| CREATE SCREEN | 23 | DELIMITED WITH | 11,18 |
| CREATE VIEW | 23 | DIF | 11,19 |
| CREATE VIEW FROM | | DIR | 25 |
| ENVIRONMENT | 24 | disk directory | 25 |
| create database | 6,20,77 | DISKSPACE | 87 |
| create index file | 33-34 | DISPLAY | 22,25 |
| create labels | 36 | DISPLAY HISTORY | 26 |
| create query file | 41 | DISPLAY MEMORY | 26 |
| create report | 50 | DISPLAY STATUS | 26,112 |
| create report form file | 22 | DISPLAY STRUCTURE | 27 |

| | | | | |
|---|---|---|---|---|
| DISPLAY USERS | 112 | EXP | 89 |
| display expressions | 7,8 | exponentiation | 89 |
| display records | 25 | EXPORT | 31 |
| display status | 26 | expressions | 122 |
| display variables | 46 | | |
| DO | 27,39 | .F. (false) | 5,28,84 |
| DO CASE | 28 | FIELD | 89 |
| DO WHILE | 28-29,30 | field delimiters | 60 |
| DO...WITH | 46 | field list | 63-64 |
| DOS commands | 7,25,52 | FIELDDEC | 18 |
| DOUBLE | 10 | FIELDLEN | 18 |
| DOW | 87 | FIELDNAME | 18 |
| DTOC | 88 | FIELDS | 12,14 |
| duplicate database structure | 17 | fields | 122-123 |
| duplicate file | 17 | FIELDTYPE | 18 |
| | | FILE | 89 |
| ECHO output | 59 | FIND | 31 |
| EDIT | 29 | FKLABEL | 90 |
| edit field | 14,111 | FKMAX | 90 |
| edit record | 14,29,111 | .FMT | 125 |
| EJECT | 29 | FOR or WHILE | 5,12 |
| ELSE | 32 | FORM | 36 |
| end application | 14 | FORMAT | 16 |
| end of field | 58 | format file | 65,124 |
| end of file | 88 | formatting | 7,8-10 |
| ENDDO | 28,30,39 | formfeed | 29 |
| environment | 91 | FOUND | 90 |
| EOF | 88 | FREEZE | 13 |
| EOF | 100 | .FRM | 126 |
| ERASE | 30 | function keys | 65-66,90 |
| ERROR | 88 | functions | 9,82-110 |
| error codes | 88,130-133 | | |
| error trapping | 44 | @...GET | 8-10,15,48 |
| ESC key | 45,62 | GETENV | 91 |
| exact comparison | 63 | global variables | 47 |
| EXCEPT | 49 | GO | 31 |
| execute program | 13,27 | GOTO | 31 |
| EXIT | 30 | GROUPS | 22 |
| exit dBase | 47 | | |

| HEADING | 50 | LIST HISTORY | 37 |
| HELP | 32 | LIST MEMORY | 37 |
| help prompt | 66 | LIST STATUS | 38,112-113 |
| hide deleted records | 60 | LIST STRUCTURE | 38 |
| history buffer | 26,37 | list records | 36 |
| | | LOAD | 39 |
| IF | 32 | local variables | 46 |
| IF SET DELETED ON | 18 | LOCATE | 16,22,39 |
| IIF | 91 | LOCK | 13 |
| immediate IF | 91 | LOG | 95 |
| IMPORT | 33 | logical fields | 122 |
| INDEX | 13,16,33 | logical operators | 120 |
| index file | 33,48,68 | LOGOUT | 113 |
| INKEY | 91-92 | LOOP | 39 |
| INPUT | 34 | LOWER | 95 |
| input buffer | 75 | LTRIM | 96 |
| INSERT | 34 | LUPDATE | 96 |
| insert record | 34 | | |
| INT | 92 | machine language | 13,39 |
| integer | 92 | macros | 82 |
| inverse field | 68 | mark record | 24 |
| ISALPHA | 93 | mask file | 42 |
| ISCOLOR | 93 | MASTER | 52 |
| ISLOWER | 93 | mathematical operators | 119 |
| ISUPPER | 94 | MAX | 96 |
| | | .MEM | 125 |
| JOIN | 35 | memo fields | 43,122 |
| | | memo width | 69 |
| key trap | 45 | menu system | 12 |
| keyboard input | 34 | MESSAGE | 97 |
| | | MIN | 97 |
| LABEL FORM | 36 | MOD | 97 |
| label file | 20,36,40,125 | MODIFY | 23,43 |
| LAST | 26,37 | MODIFY COMMAND | 40 |
| .LBL | 40,125 | MODIFY LABEL | 40 |
| LEFT | 94 | MODIFY QUERY | 41 |
| LEN | 95 | MODIFY REPORT | 42 |
| LIKE | 49 | MODIFY SCREEN | 42-43 |
| LIST | 36 | MODIFY STRUCTURE | 43 |

| | | | |
|---|---|---|---|
| MODIFY VIEW | 43-44 | position record pointer | 31 |
| MODULE | 49 | .PRG | 125 |
| MONTH | 98 | printing | 29,62,68, |
| | | | 71-72,99,115,116 |
| .NDX | 124 | PRIVATE | 46 |
| NDX | 98 | PROCEDURE | 16,47 |
| NEST | 21,41 | procedure file | 72,125 |
| network commands | 111-117 | PROW | 99 |
| NOAPPEND | 13 | PUBLIC | 47 |
| NOEJECT | 50 | | |
| NOFOLLOW | 13 | query file | 21,41,64,125 |
| NOMENU | 13 | .QRY | 125 |
| .NOT. | 120 | QUIT | 47 |
| NOTE | 44 | | |
| numeric fields | 122-123 | RANDOM | 79 |
| numeric value | 82 | RANGE | 8 |
| | | READ | 15,48 |
| odometer | 70 | READKEY | 99-100 |
| OFF | 36 | rebuild index file | 48 |
| ON ERROR | 44 | RECALL | 48 |
| ON ESCAPE | 45 | RECCOUNT | 101 |
| ON KEY | 45 | RECNO | 101 |
| open database | 81 | record count | 101 |
| operating system | 98 | record length | 102 |
| operator priority | 120-121 | record pointer | 31,76 |
| operators | 119-121 | RECSIZE | 102 |
| OPTIONS | 22 | REINDEX | 48 |
| .OR. | 120 | RELATE | 23,44 |
| OS | 98 | RELEASE | 49 |
| OTHERWISE | 28 | remove records | 45 |
| output device | 61,62 | RENAME | 49 |
| | | repeat commands | 28-29 |
| PACK | 45 | REPLACE | 50 |
| PARAMETERS | 46 | REPLICATE | 102 |
| parameters | 81 | replicate string | 102 |
| PCOL | 99 | REPORT | 50-51 |
| PFS | 30 | report form files | 22,42,126 |
| PICTURE | 8,107 | RESTORE | 51 |
| PLAIN | 50 | RESUME | 51 |

| | | | | |
|---|---|---|---|---|
| resume search | 16 | SET DEFAULT TO | 59 |
| RETRY | 51,113 | SET DELETED | 60 |
| RETURN | 52 | SET DELIMITERS | 60 |
| RIGHT | 103 | SET DELIMITERS TO | 61 |
| ROUND | 103 | SET DEVICE TO | 61 |
| rounding numbers | 103 | SET DOHISTORY | 61 |
| ROW | 104 | SET ECHO | 59,62 |
| RTRIM | 104 | SET ENCRYPTION | 114 |
| RUN | 52 | SET ESCAPE | 62 |
| | | SET EXACT | 63 |
| SAMPLE | 36 | SET EXCLUSIVE | 114 |
| SAVE | 52 | SET FIELDS | 15,63 |
| save variables | 52 | SET FIELDS TO | 63-64 |
| @...SAY | 8-10 | SET FILTER | 41 |
| .SCR | 124 | SET FILTER TO | 64 |
| screen border | 10 | SET FIXED | 65 |
| screen display | 58 | SET FORMAT TO | 65 |
| screen files | 125 | SET FUNCTION TO | 65-66 |
| SDF | 11,19 | SET HEADING | 66 |
| search | 16,39,90 | SET HELP | 66 |
| search path | 71 | SET HISTORY | 67 |
| SEEK | 53 | SET HISTORY TO | 67 |
| SELECT | 53 | SET INDEX TO | 68 |
| SET | 53 | SET INTENSITY | 68 |
| SET ALTERNATE | 54 | SET MARGIN TO | 68 |
| SET ALTERNATE TO | 54 | SET MEMOWIDTH TO | 69 |
| SET BELL | 54 | SET MENU ON | OFF | 69 |
| SET CARRY | 55 | SET MESSAGE TO | 69 |
| SET CARRY ON | 34 | SET ODOMETER TO | 70 |
| SET CATALOG | 55 | SET ORDER TO | 70 |
| SET CATALOG TO | 55 | SET PATH TO | 71 |
| SET CENTURY | 56 | SET PRINT | 71 |
| SET COLOR | 56 | SET PRINTER | 115-116 |
| SET COLOR TO | 56-57 | SET PRINTER TO | 71-72 |
| SET CONFIRM | 58 | SET PROCEDURE TO | 72 |
| SET CONSOLE | 58 | SET RELATION TO | 72-73 |
| SET DATE | 58-59 | SET SAFETY | 73 |
| SET DEBUG | 59 | SET SCOREBOARD | 73 |
| SET DECIMALS TO | 59 | SET STATUS | 74 |

| | | | | |
|---|---|---|---|---|
| SET STEP | 74 | totals file | | 79 |
| SET TALK | 74 | TRANSFORM | | 107-108 |
| SET TITLE | 75 | TRIM | | 108 |
| SET TYPEAHEAD TO | 75 | .TXT | | 11 |
| SET UNIQUE | 75 | TYPE | | 80,109 |
| SET UP | 23 | | | |
| SET VIEW TO | 76 | UNIQUE | | 34 |
| single-step mode | 74 | unique keys | | 75 |
| SKIP | 76 | UNLOCK | | 116 |
| SORT | 77 | UPDATE | | 80 |
| sorting | 77 | UPPER | | 109 |
| SPACE | 104 | USE | | 10,81 |
| SQRT | 105 | USE EXCLUSIVE | | 116 |
| square root | 105 | user message | | 69 |
| status | 26,38,73,74,112 | | | |
| stop program | 78 | VAL | | 110 |
| STORE | 77 | variables | | 37,46,77,123 |
| STR | 105 | VERSION | | 110 |
| string length | 95 | VIEW | | 23 |
| string operators | 120 | view file | | 43-44,76,126 |
| structure file | 20 | .VUE | | 23,126 |
| STUFF | 105 | | | |
| SUBSTR | 106 | WAIT | | 81 |
| SUM | 78 | WHILE | | 5 |
| SUMMARY | 51 | WIDTH | | 13 |
| SUSPEND | 78 | WITH | | 27 |
| SYLK | 11,19 | WKS | | 11,19 |
| syntax conventions | 2-3 | work environment | | 24 |
| | | | | |
| .T. (true) | 84 | YEAR | | 109 |
| TEDIT | 40 | | | |
| template symbols | 9,108 | ZAP | | 81 |
| TEXT | 79 | | | |
| text files | 126 | | | |
| TIME | 106 | | | |
| title prompt | 75 | | | |
| @...TO | 10 | | | |
| TO PRINT | 6 | | | |
| TOTAL | 79 | | | |

# *Quick* Program Reference Guides

The Program Reference Guide series from Abacus gives busy people like you the essential PC information you need—right now.

These lightweight, convenient books are designed specifically to give you lightning-fast access to the most popular PC software. It's *instant information at your fingertips.*

*Concise*
- PRG's easily fit in your coat pocket or purse— and take up a lot less space on your desk than all those user manuals, books & binders.

*Portable*
- Have a PC at home, as well as the office? Slip a PRG (or two, or three...) into your briefcase. Leave those heavy reference books up on the shelf.

*Light-weight*
- Have a laptop PC? Slip a couple of PRG's into the computer's carrying case. But don't try this with your user's manuals.

*Durable*
- PRG's are hardcover books that stand up to heavy daily use. And PRG's are priced right at $9.95 each.

You'll find our little Program Reference Guides are indispensible. That's why we're writing them for all of the major PC application software packages.

Try one. You'll be back for more.

## MS-DOS
Describes all of the DOS
commands through
version 3.2; lists para-
meters, options, and
syntax. Complete
sections on batch files,
configuration, more.

**Microsoft**
## Word
Concise, tightly organized
guide to Word's menus,
commands, command
fields, options, shortcuts,
and the mouse. Complete
sections on advanced
features—form letters,
indexing, and more.

**Microsoft**
## GW-BASIC
Complete description of
the BASIC commands,
syntax and parameters at a
glance.

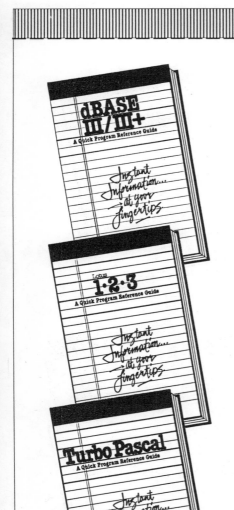

### dBASE III/III+
Complete guide listing
commands with syntax,
options, and description
of their use.

### Lotus
## 1 - 2 - 3
Quick access to 1-2-3
commands, options,
more. Essential reference
for any 1-2-3 user.

### Turbo Pascal
Handy reference of
Turbo's reserved words,
parameters, syntax and
keywords.

Other titles
available soon:

**Multiplan**

**Wordstar**

**Word Perfect**

and more coming

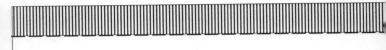

# Order Info
## for Program Reference Guides

- Each Program Reference Guide is available from more than 2000 dealers and bookstores in the U.S. and Canada. To find out the dealer location nearest to you call

## (616) 698-0330
8:30 am-8:00 pm Eastern Standard Time

- If they don't stock the PRG you're looking for, order from us directly by phone. We accept Mastercard, Visa and American Express.

For *extra-fast* 24-hour shipment service, order by phone with your credit card

**Abacus**
**P.O. Box 318**
**Grand Rapids, MI  49588**

Phone: (616) 698-0330          Telex: 709-101

# ⦙⦙⦙⦙⦙⦙⦙⦙ Order Blank ⦙⦙⦙⦙⦙⦙⦙⦙

Name: _____

Address: _____

City: _____ State: _____ Zip: _____

Phone: _____ / _____ Country: _____

| Qty | Title | Price |
|-----|-------|-------|
| | | $9.95 |
| | | $9.95 |
| | | $9.95 |
| | | $9.95 |
| | | $9.95 |
| | | $9.95 |
| **Mich. residents add 4% sales tax** | | |
| **Shipping/Handling charge** (Foreign Orders $4.00 per item) | | $2.00 |
| **Check/M.O.      TOTAL enclosed** | | |

Credit Card#

| | | | | | | | | | | | | | | | | | | | |
|-|-|-|-|-|-|-|-|-|-|-|-|-|-|-|-|-|-|-|-|

Expiration date  *Cardholder Signature*

| | | | |
|-|-|-|-|

Send your completed order blank to:

### Abacus
### P.O. Box 318
### Grand Rapids, MI  49588

Your order will be shipped within 24 hours our receiving it.
**For extra-fast 24-hour shipment service, order by
phone with your credit card—call (616) 698-0330.**